We Are the Builders
of Our Fortunes

*Visit our website for more of
the greatest success guides ever written*
www.SuccessBooks.net

As a Man Thinketh by James Allen
Think and Grow Rich by Napoleon Hill
The Science of Getting Rich by Wallace D. Wattles
The Way to Wealth by Benjamin Franklin
A Message to Garcia by Elbert Hubbard
The Art of War by Sun Tzu

Copyright © 2013 Best Success Books
Printed in the USA

We Are the Builders of Our Fortunes

Success through Self-Reliance

Ralph Waldo Emerson

EDITED BY
CHARLES CONRAD

BEST SUCCESS BOOKS

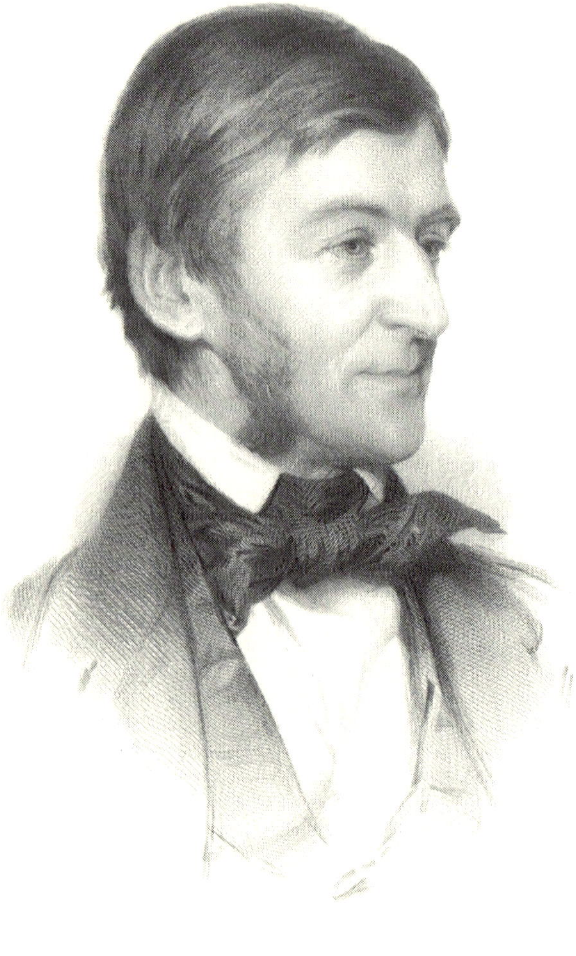

CONTENTS

Introduction by Charles Conrad	1
SELF-RELIANCE	3
GREATNESS	29
COURAGE	41
INSPIRATION	55
RESOURCES	71
SUCCESS	81
POWER	99
WEALTH	117
SINCERITY	141
COMPENSATION	147

Introduction

RALPH WALDO EMERSON (1803–1882) was the grandfather of the modern self-development movement. In the 150 years since he wrote his essays and travelled the country lecturing, Emerson's central messages—the power of thought, individual self-reliance, harmony with nature, and the unity of all things—have only grown in influence.

James Allen, author of *As a Man Thinketh*, said, "Every young person ought to read Emerson's essay on 'Self-Reliance.' It is the manliest, most virile essay that was ever penned."

Wallace D. Wattles, in *The Science of Getting Rich*, wrote, "The reader who would dig to the philosophical foundations of this is advised to read Emerson for himself."

Elbert Hubbard, author of *A Message to Garcia*, called Emerson "our modern Plato," adding, "Every time I pick up a volume of Emerson, I have to reach for my notepad and pencil."

And Napoleon Hill, in his classic *Think and Grow Rich*, referred to Emerson as a "genius of outstanding achievement."

Through these early disciples, Emerson's philosophy was passed down to today's inspirational leaders, such as Tony Robbins, Wayne Dyer, Rhonda Byrne, Oprah Winfrey, and many others.

The volume you are holding is the first-ever collection of Emerson's writings on the theme of Success. I wish to rescue Emerson from the English department and present the *practical* side of his philosophy. These essays are not simply beautifully-written, historically-important literary pieces—they are powerful, provocative teachings that can transform your life *today*.

In these pages, Emerson will teach you:

- How to find and follow your inner genius;
- How your thoughts shape your reality;
- Where to find inspiration;
- Why wealth is a mental and moral phenomena;
- Why economies rise or fall;
- What defines human greatness;
and much more.

Every great enterprise, invention, or adventure first begins as an *idea*. Ideas are the most powerful tools on earth—when you know how to grasp, organize, and use them. Reading Emerson will increase your storehouse of ideas, and train you to organize your thoughts and put them to good use.

I hope you'll spend a little time with Emerson each morning. Begin a regular practice of reading a few pages while you sip your morning coffee, then take a walk to meditate upon them. His words will enlighten, entertain, and enrich you. You'll be surprised at the increasing quality and quantity of your own ideas!

Success is the sure result of successful thinking. And by reading Emerson, you'll learn to think successfully.

—CHARLES CONRAD

Self-Reliance

Ne te quaesiveris extra.
("Do not seek yourself outside yourself.")

I READ THE OTHER DAY some verses written by an eminent painter which were original and not conventional. The soul always hears an admonition in such lines, let the subject be what it may. The sentiment they instill is of more value than any thought they may contain. To believe your own thought, to believe that what is true for you in your private heart is true for all men,—that is genius. Speak your latent conviction, and it shall be the universal sense; for the inmost in due time becomes the outmost,—and our first thought is rendered back to us by the trumpets of the Last Judgment. Familiar as the voice of the mind is to each, the highest merit we ascribe to Moses, Plato, and Milton is, that they set at naught books and traditions, and spoke not what men but what *they* thought. A man should learn to detect and watch that gleam of light which flashes across his mind from within, more than the luster of the firmament of bards and sages. Yet he dismisses without notice his thought, because it is his. In every work of genius we recognize our own rejected thoughts: they come back to us with a certain alienated majesty. Great works of art have no more affecting lesson for us than this. They teach us to abide by our spontaneous impression with good-humored inflexibility then most when the whole cry of voices is on the other side. Else, tomorrow a stranger will say with masterly good sense precisely what we have thought and felt all the time, and we shall be forced to take with shame our own opinion from another.

There is a time in every man's education when he arrives at the conviction that envy is ignorance; that imitation is suicide; that he must take himself for better, for worse, as his portion; that though the wide universe is full of good, no kernel of nourishing corn can come to him but through his toil bestowed on that plot of ground which is given to him to till. The power which resides in him is new in nature, and none but he knows what that is which he can do, nor does he know until he has tried. Not for nothing one face, one character, one fact, makes much impression on him, and another none. This sculpture in the memory is not without pre-established harmony. The eye was placed where one ray should fall, that it might testify of that particular ray. We but half express ourselves, and are ashamed of that divine idea which each of us represents. It may be safely trusted as proportionate and of good issues, so it be faithfully imparted, but God will not have his work made manifest by cowards. A man is relieved and gay when he has put his heart into his work and done his best; but what he has said or done otherwise, shall give him no peace. It is a deliverance which does not deliver. In the attempt his genius deserts him; no muse befriends; no invention, no hope.

Trust thyself: every heart vibrates to that iron string. Accept the place the divine providence has found for you, the society of your contemporaries, the connection of events. Great men have always done so, and confided themselves childlike to the genius of their age, betraying their perception that the absolutely trustworthy was seated at their heart, working through their hands, predominating in all their being. And we are now men, and must accept in the highest mind the same transcendent destiny; and not minors and invalids in a protected corner, not cowards fleeing before a revolution, but guides, redeemers, and benefactors, obeying the Almighty effort, and advancing on Chaos and the Dark.

What pretty oracles nature yields us on this text, in the face and behavior of children, babes, and even brutes! That divided and rebel mind, that distrust of a sentiment because our arithmetic has computed the strength and means opposed to our purpose, these have not. Their mind being whole, their eye is as yet unconquered, and when we look in their faces, we are disconcerted. Infancy conforms to nobody: all conform to it, so that one babe commonly makes four or five out of the adults who prattle and play to it. So God has armed youth and puberty and manhood no less with its own piquancy and charm, and made it enviable and gracious and its claims not to be put by, if it will stand by itself. Do not think the youth has no force, because he cannot speak to you and me. Hark! in the next room his voice is sufficiently clear and emphatic. It seems he knows how to speak to his contemporaries. Bashful or bold, then, he will know how to make us seniors very unnecessary.

The nonchalance of boys who are sure of a dinner, and would disdain as much as a lord to do or say aught to conciliate one, is the healthy attitude of human nature. A boy is in the parlor what the pit is in the playhouse; independent, irresponsible, looking out from his corner on such people and facts as pass by, he tries and sentences them on their merits, in the swift, summary way of boys, as good, bad, interesting, silly, eloquent, troublesome. He cumbers himself never about consequences, about interests: he gives an independent, genuine verdict. You must court him: he does not court you. But the man is, as it were, clapped into jail by his consciousness. As soon as he has once acted or spoken with *éclat*, he is a committed person, watched by the sympathy or the hatred of hundreds, whose affections must now enter into his account. There is no Lethe for this. Ah, that he could pass again into his neutrality! Who can thus avoid all pledges, and having observed, observe again from the same unaffected, unbiased, unbribable, unaffrighted innocence, must always be formidable. He would utter opinions on all passing affairs, which being seen to be not private, but necessary, would sink like darts into the ear of men, and put them in fear.

These are the voices which we hear in solitude, but they grow faint and inaudible as we enter into the world. Society everywhere is in conspiracy against the manhood of every one of its members. Society is a joint-stock company, in which the members agree, for the better securing of his bread to each shareholder, to surrender the liberty and culture of the eater. The virtue in most request is conformity. Self-reliance is its aversion. It loves not realities and creators, but names and customs.

Whoso would be a man must be a nonconformist. He who would gather immortal palms must not be hindered by the name of goodness, but must explore if it be goodness. Nothing is at last sacred but the integrity of your own mind. Absolve you to yourself, and you shall have the suffrage of the world. I remember an answer which when quite young I was prompted to make to a valued adviser, who was wont to importune me with the dear old doctrines of the church. On my saying, "What have I to do with the sacredness of traditions, if I live wholly from within?" my friend suggested,—"But these impulses may be from below, not from above." I replied, "They do not seem to me to be such; but if I am the Devil's child, I will live then from the Devil." No law can be sacred to me but that of my nature. Good and bad are but names very readily transferable to that or this; the only right is what is after my constitution, the only wrong what is against it. A man is to carry himself in the presence of all opposition, as if every thing were titular and ephemeral but he. I am ashamed to think how easily we capitulate to badges and names, to large societies and dead institutions. Every decent and well-spoken individual affects and sways me more than is right. I ought to go upright and vital, and speak the rude truth in all ways. If malice and vanity wear the coat of philanthropy, shall that pass? If an angry bigot assumes this bountiful cause of Abolition, and comes to me with his last news from Barbadoes, why should I not say to him, 'Go love thy infant; love thy wood-chopper: be good-natured and modest: have that grace; and never varnish your hard, uncharitable ambition with this incredible tenderness for black folk a thousand miles off. Thy love afar is spite at home.' Rough and graceless would be such greeting, but truth is handsomer than the affectation of love. Your goodness must have some edge to it,—else it is none. The doctrine of hatred must be preached as the counteraction of the doctrine of love when that pules and whines. I shun father and mother and wife and brother, when my genius calls me. I would write on the lintels of the door-post, *Whim*. I hope it is somewhat better than whim at last, but we cannot spend the day in explanation. Expect me not to show cause why I seek or why I exclude company. Then, again, do not tell me, as a good man did today, of my obligation to put all poor men in good situations. Are they my poor? I tell thee, thou foolish philanthropist, that I grudge the dollar, the dime, the cent, I give to such men as do not belong to me and to whom I do not belong. There is a class of persons to whom by all spiritual affinity I am bought and sold; for them I will go to prison, if need be; but your miscellaneous popular charities; the education at college of fools; the building of meeting-houses to the vain end to which many now stand; alms to sots; and the thousandfold Relief Societies;—though I confess with shame I sometimes succumb and give the dollar, it is a wicked dollar which by and by I shall have the manhood to withhold.

Virtues are, in the popular estimate, rather the exception than the rule. There is the man *and* his virtues. Men do what is called a good action, as some piece of courage or charity, much as they would pay a fine in expiation of daily non-appearance on parade. Their works are done as an apology or extenuation of their living in the world,—as invalids and the insane pay a high board. Their virtues are penances. I do not wish to expiate, but to live. My life is for itself and not for a spectacle. I much prefer that it should be of a lower strain, so it be genuine and equal, than that it should be glittering and unsteady. I wish it to be sound and sweet, and not to need diet and bleeding. I ask primary evidence that you are a man, and refuse this appeal from the man to his actions. I know that for myself it makes no difference whether I do or forbear those actions which are reckoned excellent. I cannot consent to pay for a privilege where I have intrinsic right. Few and mean as my gifts may be, I actually am, and do not need for my own assurance or the assurance of my fellows any secondary testimony.

What I must do is all that concerns me, not what the people think. This rule, equally arduous in actual and in intellectual life, may serve for the whole distinction between greatness and meanness. It is the harder, because you will always find those who think they know what is your duty better than you know it. It is easy in the world to live after the world's opinion; it is easy in solitude to live after our own; but the great man is he who in the midst of the crowd keeps with perfect sweetness the independence of solitude.

The objection to conforming to usages that have become dead to you is, that it scatters your force. It loses your time and blurs the impression of your character. If you maintain a dead church, contribute to a dead Bible-society, vote with a great party either for the government or against it, spread your table like base housekeepers,—under all these screens I have difficulty to detect the precise man you are. And, of course, so much force is withdrawn from your proper life. But do your work, and I shall know you. Do your work, and you shall reinforce yourself. A man must consider what a blindman's-buff is this game of conformity. If I know your sect, I anticipate your argument. I hear a preacher announce for his text and topic the expediency of one of the institutions of his church. Do I not know beforehand that not possibly can he say a new and spontaneous word? Do I not know that, with all this ostentation of examining the grounds of the institution, he will do no such thing? Do I not know that he is pledged to himself not to look but at one side,—the permitted side, not as a man, but as a parish minister? He is a retained attorney, and these airs of the bench are the emptiest affectation. Well, most men have bound their eyes with one or another handkerchief, and attached themselves to some one of these communities of opinion. This conformity makes them not false in a few particulars, authors of a few lies, but false in all particulars. Their every truth is not quite true. Their two is not the real two, their four not the real four; so that every word they say chagrins us, and we know not where to begin to set them right. Meantime nature is not slow to equip us in the prison-uniform of the party to which we adhere. We come to wear one cut of face and figure, and acquire by degrees the gentlest asinine expression. There is a mortifying experience in particular, which does not fail to wreak itself also in the general history; I mean "the foolish face of praise," the forced smile which we put on in company where we do not feel at ease in answer to conversation which does not interest us. The muscles, not spontaneously moved, but moved by a low usurping willfulness, grow tight about the outline of the face with the most disagreeable sensation.

For nonconformity the world whips you with its displeasure. And therefore a man must know how to estimate a sour face. The by-standers look askance on him in the public street or in the friend's parlor. If this aversion had its origin in contempt and resistance like his own, he might well go home with a sad countenance; but the sour faces of the multitude, like their sweet faces, have no deep cause, but are put on and off as the wind blows and a newspaper directs. Yet is the discontent of the multitude more formidable than that of the senate and the college. It is easy enough for a firm man who knows the world to brook the rage of the cultivated classes. Their rage is decorous and prudent, for they are timid as being very vulnerable themselves. But when to their feminine rage the indignation of the people is added, when the ignorant and the poor are aroused, when the unintelligent brute force that lies at the bottom of society is made to growl and mow, it needs the habit of magnanimity and religion to treat it godlike as a trifle of no concernment.

The other terror that scares us from self-trust is our consistency; a reverence for our past act or word, because the eyes of others have no other data for computing our orbit than our past acts, and we are loath to disappoint them.

But why should you keep your head over your shoulder? Why drag about this corpse of your memory, lest you contradict somewhat you have stated in this or that public place? Suppose you should contradict yourself; what then? It seems to be a rule of wisdom never to rely on your memory alone, scarcely even in acts of pure memory, but to bring the past for judgment into the thousand-eyed present, and live ever in a new day. In your metaphysics you have denied personality to the Deity: yet when the devout motions of the soul come, yield to them heart and life, though they should clothe God with shape and color. Leave your theory, as Joseph his coat in the hand of the harlot, and flee.

A foolish consistency is the hobgoblin of little minds, adored by little statesmen and philosophers and divines. With consistency a great soul has simply nothing to do. He may as well concern himself with his shadow on the wall. Speak what you think now in hard words, and tomorrow speak what tomorrow thinks in hard words again, though it contradict every thing you said today.—'Ah, so you shall be sure to be misunderstood.'— Is it so bad, then, to be misunderstood? Pythagoras was misunderstood, and Socrates, and Jesus, and Luther, and Copernicus, and Galileo, and

Newton, and every pure and wise spirit that ever took flesh. To be great is to be misunderstood.

I suppose no man can violate his nature. All the sallies of his will are rounded in by the law of his being, as the inequalities of Andes and Himmaleh are insignificant in the curve of the sphere. Nor does it matter how you gauge and try him. A character is like an acrostic or Alexandrian stanza;—read it forward, backward, or across, it still spells the same thing. In this pleasing, contrite wood-life which God allows me, let me record day by day my honest thought without prospect or retrospect, and, I cannot doubt, it will be found symmetrical, though I mean it not, and see it not. My book should smell of pines and resound with the hum of insects. The swallow over my window should interweave that thread or straw he carries in his bill into my web also. We pass for what we are. Character teaches above our wills. Men imagine that they communicate their virtue or vice only by overt actions, and do not see that virtue or vice emit a breath every moment.

There will be an agreement in whatever variety of actions, so they be each honest and natural in their hour. For of one will, the actions will be harmonious, however unlike they seem. These varieties are lost sight of at a little distance, at a little height of thought. One tendency unites them all. The voyage of the best ship is a zigzag line of a hundred tacks. See the line from a sufficient distance, and it straightens itself to the average tendency. Your genuine action will explain itself, and will explain your other genuine actions. Your conformity explains nothing. Act singly, and what you have already done singly will justify you now. Greatness appeals to the future. If I can be firm enough today to do right, and scorn eyes, I must have done so much right before as to defend me now. Be it how it will, do right now. Always scorn appearances, and you always may. The force of character is cumulative. All the foregone days of virtue work their health into this. What makes the majesty of the heroes of the senate and the field, which so fills the imagination? The consciousness of a train of great days and victories behind. They shed an united light on the advancing actor. He is attended as by a visible escort of angels. That is it which throws thunder into Chatham's voice, and dignity into Washington's port, and America into Adams's eye. Honor is venerable to us because it is no ephemeris. It is always ancient virtue. We worship it today because it is not of today. We love it and pay it homage, because it is not a trap for our love and homage, but is self-dependent, self-derived, and therefore of an old immaculate pedigree, even if shown in a young person.

I hope in these days we have heard the last of conformity and consistency. Let the words be gazetted and ridiculous henceforward. Instead of the gong for dinner, let us hear a whistle from the Spartan fife. Let us never bow and apologize more. A great man is coming to eat at my house. I do not wish to please him; I wish that he should wish to please me. I will stand here for humanity, and though I would make it kind, I would make it true. Let us affront and reprimand the smooth mediocrity and squalid contentment of the times, and hurl in the face of custom, and trade, and office, the fact which is the upshot of all history, that there is a great responsible Thinker and Actor working wherever a man works; that a true man belongs to no other time or place, but is the centre of things. Where he is, there is nature. He measures you, and all men, and all events. Ordinarily, every body in society reminds us of somewhat else, or of some other person. Character, reality, reminds you of nothing else; it takes place of the whole creation. The man must be so much, that he must make all circumstances indifferent. Every true man is a cause, a country, and an age; requires infinite spaces and numbers and time fully to accomplish his design;—and posterity seem to follow his steps as a train of clients. A man Caesar is born, and for ages after we have a Roman Empire. Christ is born, and millions of minds so grow and cleave to his genius, that he is confounded with virtue and the possible of man. An institution is the lengthened shadow of one man; as, Monachism, of the Hermit Antony; the Reformation, of Luther; Quakerism, of Fox; Methodism, of Wesley; Abolition, of Clarkson. Scipio, Milton called "the height of Rome"; and all history resolves itself very easily into the biography of a few stout and earnest persons.

Let a man then know his worth, and keep things under his feet. Let him not peep or steal, or skulk up and down with the air of a charity-boy, a bastard, or an interloper, in the world which exists for him. But the man in the street, finding no worth in himself which corresponds to the force which built a tower or sculptured a marble god, feels poor when he looks on these. To him a palace, a statue, or a costly book have an alien and forbidding air, much like a gay equipage, and seem to say like that, 'Who are you, Sir?' Yet they all are his, suitors for his notice, petitioners to his faculties that they will come out and take possession. The picture waits for my verdict: it is not to command me, but I am to settle its claims to praise. That popular fable of the sot who was picked up dead drunk in the street, carried to the duke's house, washed and dressed and laid in the duke's bed, and, on his waking, treated with all obsequious ceremony like the duke, and assured that he had been insane, owes its popularity to the fact, that it symbolizes so well the state of man, who is in the world a sort of sot, but now and then wakes up, exercises his reason, and finds himself a true prince.

Our reading is mendicant and sycophantic. In history, our imagination plays us false. Kingdom and lordship, power and estate, are a gaudier vocabulary than private John and Edward in a small house and common day's work; but the things of life are the same to both; the sum total of both is the same. Why all this deference to Alfred, and Scanderbeg, and Gustavus? Suppose they were virtuous; did they wear out virtue? As great a stake depends on your private act today, as followed their public and renowned steps. When private men shall act with original views, the luster will be transferred from the actions of kings to those of gentlemen.

The world has been instructed by its kings, who have so magnetized the eyes of nations. It has been taught by this colossal symbol the mutual reverence that is due from man to man. The joyful loyalty with which men have everywhere suffered the king, the noble, or the great proprietor to walk among them by a law of his own, make his own scale of men and things, and reverse theirs, pay for benefits not with money but with honor, and represent the law in his person, was the hieroglyphic by which they obscurely signified their consciousness of their own right and comeliness, the right of every man.

The magnetism which all original action exerts is explained when we inquire the reason of self-trust. Who is the Trustee? What is the aboriginal Self, on which a universal reliance may be grounded? What is the nature and power of that science-baffling star, without parallax, without calculable elements, which shoots a ray of beauty even into trivial and impure actions, if the least mark of independence appear? The inquiry leads us to that source, at once the essence of genius, of virtue, and of life, which we call Spontaneity or Instinct. We denote this primary wisdom as Intuition, whilst all later teachings are tuitions. In that deep force, the last fact behind which analysis cannot go, all things find their common origin. For, the sense of being which in calm hours rises, we know not how, in the soul, is not diverse from things, from space, from light, from time, from man, but one with them, and proceeds obviously from the same source whence their life and being also proceed. We first share the life by which things exist, and afterwards see them as appearances in nature, and forget that we have shared their cause. Here is the fountain of action and of thought. Here are the lungs of that inspiration which giveth man wisdom, and which cannot be denied without impiety and atheism. We lie in the lap of immense intelligence, which makes us receivers of its truth and organs of its activity. When we discern justice, when we discern truth, we do nothing of ourselves, but allow a passage to its beams. If we ask whence this comes, if we seek to pry into the soul that causes, all philosophy is at fault. Its presence or its absence is all we can affirm. Every man discriminates between the voluntary acts of his mind, and his involuntary perceptions, and knows that to his involuntary perceptions a perfect faith is due. He may err in the expression of them, but he knows that these things are so, like day and night, not to be disputed. My willful actions and acquisitions are but roving;—the idlest reverie, the faintest native emotion, command my curiosity and respect. Thoughtless people contradict as readily the statement of perceptions as of opinions, or rather much more readily; for, they do not distinguish between perception and notion. They fancy that I choose to see this or that thing. But perception is not whimsical, but fatal. If I see a trait, my children will see it after me, and in course of time, all mankind,—although it may chance that no one has seen it before me. For my perception of it is as much a fact as the sun.

The relations of the soul to the divine spirit are so pure, that it is profane to seek to interpose helps. It must be that when God speaketh he should communicate, not one thing, but all things; should fill the world with his voice; should scatter forth light, nature, time, souls, from the centre of the present thought; and new date and new create the whole. Whenever a mind is simple, and receives a divine wisdom, old things pass away,—means, teachers, texts, temples fall; it lives now, and absorbs past and future into the present hour. All things are made sacred by relation to it,—one as much as another. All things are dissolved to their centre by their cause, and, in the universal miracle, petty and particular miracles disappear. If, therefore, a man claims to know and speak of God, and carries you backward to the phraseology of some old moldered nation in another country, in another world, believe him not. Is the acorn better than the oak which is its fulness and completion? Is the parent better than the child into whom he has cast his ripened being? Whence, then, this worship of the past? The centuries are conspirators against the sanity and authority of the soul. Time and space are but physiological colors which the eye makes, but the soul is light; where it is, is day; where it was, is night; and history is an impertinence and an injury, if it be any thing more than a cheerful apologue or parable of my being and becoming.

Man is timid and apologetic; he is no longer upright; he dares not say 'I think,' 'I am,' but quotes some saint or sage. He is ashamed before the blade of grass or the blowing rose. These roses under my window make no reference to former roses or to better ones; they are for what they are; they exist with God today. There is no time to them. There is simply the rose; it is perfect in every moment of its existence. Before a leaf-bud has burst, its whole life acts; in the full-blown flower there is no more; in the leafless root there is no less. Its nature is satisfied, and it satisfies nature, in all moments alike. But man postpones or remembers; he does not live in the present, but with reverted eye laments the past, or, heedless of the riches that surround him, stands on tiptoe to foresee the future. He cannot be happy and strong until he too lives with nature in the present, above time.

This should be plain enough. Yet see what strong intellects dare not yet hear God himself, unless he speak the phraseology of I know not what David, or Jeremiah, or Paul. We shall not always set so great a price on a few texts, on a few lives. We are like children who repeat by rote the sentences of grandames and tutors, and, as they grow older, of the men of talents and character they chance to see,—painfully recollecting the exact words they spoke; afterwards, when they come into the point of view which those had who uttered these sayings, they understand them, and are willing to let the words go; for, at any time, they can use words as good when occasion comes. If we live truly, we shall see truly. It is as easy for the strong man to be strong, as it is for the weak to be weak. When we have new perception, we shall gladly disburden the memory of its hoarded treasures as old rubbish. When a man lives with God, his voice shall be as sweet as the murmur of the brook and the rustle of the corn.

And now at last the highest truth on this subject remains unsaid; probably cannot be said; for all that we say is the far-off remembering of the intuition. That thought, by what I can now nearest approach to say it, is this. When good is near you, when you have life in yourself, it is not by any known or accustomed way; you shall not discern the foot-prints of any other; you shall not see the face of man; you shall not hear any name;—the way, the thought, the good, shall be wholly strange and new. It shall exclude example and experience. You take the way from man, not to man. All persons that ever existed are its forgotten ministers. Fear and hope are alike beneath it. There is somewhat low even in hope. In the hour of vision, there is nothing that can be called gratitude, nor properly joy. The soul raised over passion beholds identity and eternal causation, perceives the self-existence of Truth and Right, and calms itself with knowing that all things go well. Vast spaces of nature, the Atlantic Ocean, the South Sea,— long intervals of time, years, centuries,—are of no account. This which I think and feel underlay every former state of life and circumstances, as it does underlie my present, and what is called life, and what is called death.

Life only avails, not the having lived. Power ceases in the instant of repose; it resides in the moment of transition from a past to a new state, in the shooting of the gulf, in the darting to an aim. This one fact the world hates, that the soul *becomes*; for that for ever degrades the past, turns all riches to poverty, all reputation to a shame, confounds the saint with the rogue, shoves Jesus and Judas equally aside. Why, then, do we prate of self-reliance? Inasmuch as the soul is present, there will be power not confident but agent. To talk of reliance is a poor external way of speaking. Speak rather of that which relies, because it works and is. Who has more obedience than I masters me, though he should not raise his finger. Round him I must revolve by the gravitation of spirits. We fancy it rhetoric, when we speak of eminent virtue. We do not yet see that virtue is Height, and that a man or a company of men, plastic and permeable to principles, by the law of nature must overpower and ride all cities, nations, kings, rich men, poets, who are not.

This is the ultimate fact which we so quickly reach on this, as on every topic, the resolution of all into the ever-blessed One. Self-existence is the attribute of the Supreme Cause, and it constitutes the measure of good by the degree in which it enters into all lower forms. All things real are so by so much virtue as they contain. Commerce, husbandry, hunting, whaling, war, eloquence, personal weight, are somewhat, and engage my respect as examples of its presence and impure action. I see the same law working in nature for conservation and growth. Power is in nature the essential measure of right. Nature suffers nothing to remain in her kingdoms which cannot help itself. The genesis and maturation of a planet, its poise and orbit, the bended tree recovering itself from the strong wind, the vital resources of every animal and vegetable, are demonstrations of the self-sufficing, and therefore self-relying soul.

Thus all concentrates: let us not rove; let us sit at home with the cause. Let us stun and astonish the intruding rabble of men and books and institutions, by a simple declaration of the divine fact. Bid the invaders take the shoes from off their feet, for God is here within. Let our simplicity judge them, and our docility to our own law demonstrate the poverty of nature and fortune beside our native riches.

But now we are a mob. Man does not stand in awe of man, nor is his genius admonished to stay at home, to put itself in communication with the internal ocean, but it goes abroad to beg a cup of water of the urns of other men. We must go alone. I like the silent church before the service begins, better than any preaching. How far off, how cool, how chaste the persons look, begirt each one with a precinct or sanctuary! So let us always sit. Why should we assume the faults of our friend, or wife, or father, or child, because they sit around our hearth, or are said to have the same blood? All men have my blood, and I have all men's. Not for that will I adopt their petulance or folly, even to the extent of being ashamed of it. But your isolation must not be mechanical, but spiritual, that is, must be elevation. At times the whole world seems to be in conspiracy to importune you with emphatic trifles. Friend, client, child, sickness, fear, want, charity, all knock at once at thy closet door, and say,—'Come out unto us.' But keep thy state; come not into their confusion. The power men possess to annoy me, I give them by a weak curiosity. No man can come near me but through my act. "What we love that we have, but by desire we bereave ourselves of the love."

If we cannot at once rise to the sanctities of obedience and faith, let us at least resist our temptations; let us enter into the state of war, and wake Thor and Woden, courage and constancy, in our Saxon breasts. This is to be done in our smooth times by speaking the truth. Check this lying hospitality and lying affection. Live no longer to the expectation of these deceived and deceiving people with whom we converse. Say to them, O father, O mother, O wife, O brother, O friend, I have lived with you after appearances hitherto. Henceforward I am the truth's. Be it known unto you that henceforward I obey no law less than the eternal law. I will have no covenants but proximities. I shall endeavor to nourish my parents, to support my family, to be the chaste husband of one wife,—but these relations I must fill after a new and unprecedented way. I appeal from your customs. I must be myself. I cannot break myself any longer for you, or you. If you can love me for what I am, we shall be the happier. If you cannot, I will still seek to deserve that you should. I will not hide my tastes or aversions. I will so trust that what is deep is holy, that I will do strongly before the sun and moon whatever inly rejoices me, and the heart appoints. If you are noble, I will love you; if you are not, I will not hurt you and myself by hypocritical attentions. If you are true, but not in the same truth with me, cleave to your companions; I will seek my own. I do this not selfishly, but humbly and truly. It is alike your interest, and mine, and all men's, however long we have dwelt in lies, to live in truth. Does this sound harsh today? You will soon love what is dictated by your nature as well as mine, and, if we follow the truth, it will bring us out safe at last.—But so you may give these friends pain. Yes, but I cannot sell my liberty and my power, to save their sensibility. Besides, all persons have their moments of reason, when they look out into the region of absolute truth; then will they justify me, and do the same thing.

The populace think that your rejection of popular standards is a rejection of all standard, and mere antinomianism; and the bold sensualist will use the name of philosophy to gild his crimes. But the law of consciousness abides. There are two confessionals, in one or the other of which we must be shriven. You may fulfill your round of duties by clearing yourself in the *direct*, or in the *reflex* way. Consider whether you have satisfied your relations to father, mother, cousin, neighbor, town, cat, and dog; whether any of these can upbraid you. But I may also neglect this reflex standard, and absolve me to myself. I have my own stern claims and perfect circle. It denies the name of duty to many offices that are called duties. But if I can discharge its debts, it enables me to dispense with the popular code. If any one imagines that this law is lax, let him keep its commandment one day.

And truly it demands something godlike in him who has cast off the common motives of humanity, and has ventured to trust himself for a taskmaster. High be his heart, faithful his will, clear his sight, that he may in good earnest be doctrine, society, law, to himself, that a simple purpose may be to him as strong as iron necessity is to others!

If any man consider the present aspects of what is called by distinction *society*, he will see the need of these ethics. The sinew and heart of man seem to be drawn out, and we are become timorous, desponding whimperers. We are afraid of truth, afraid of fortune, afraid of death, and afraid of each other. Our age yields no great and perfect persons. We want men and women who shall renovate life and our social state, but we see that most natures are insolvent, cannot satisfy their own wants, have an ambition out of all proportion to their practical force, and do lean and beg day and night continually. Our housekeeping is mendicant, our arts, our occupations, our marriages, our religion, we have not chosen, but society has chosen for us. We are parlor soldiers. We shun the rugged battle of fate, where strength is born.

If our young men miscarry in their first enterprises, they lose all heart. If the young merchant fails, men say he is *ruined*. If the finest genius studies at one of our colleges, and is not installed in an office within one year afterwards in the cities or suburbs of Boston or New York, it seems to his friends and to himself that he is right in being disheartened, and in complaining the rest of his life. A sturdy lad from New Hampshire or Vermont, who in turn tries all the professions, who *teams it, farms it, peddles,* keeps a school, preaches, edits a newspaper, goes to Congress, buys a township, and so forth, in successive years, and always, like a cat, falls on his feet, is worth a hundred of these city dolls. He walks abreast with his days, and feels no shame in not 'studying a profession,' for he does not postpone his life, but lives already. He has not one chance, but a hundred chances. Let a Stoic open the resources of man, and tell men they are not leaning willows, but can and must detach themselves; that with the exercise of self-trust, new powers shall appear; that a man is the word made flesh, born to shed healing to the nations, that he should be ashamed of our compassion, and that the moment he acts from himself, tossing the laws, the books, idolatries, and customs out of the window, we pity him no more, but thank and revere him,—and that teacher shall restore the life of man to splendor, and make his name dear to all history.

It is easy to see that a greater self-reliance must work a revolution in all the offices and relations of men; in their religion; in their education; in their pursuits; their modes of living; their association; in their property; in their speculative views.

1. In what prayers do men allow themselves! That which they call a holy office is not so much as brave and manly. Prayer looks abroad and asks for some foreign addition to come through some foreign virtue, and loses itself in endless mazes of natural and supernatural, and mediatorial and miraculous. Prayer that craves a particular commodity,—any thing less than all good,—is vicious. Prayer is the contemplation of the facts of life from the highest point of view. It is the soliloquy of a beholding and jubilant soul. It is the spirit of God pronouncing his works good. But prayer as a means to effect a private end is meanness and theft. It supposes

dualism and not unity in nature and consciousness. As soon as the man is at one with God, he will not beg. He will then see prayer in all action. The prayer of the farmer kneeling in his field to weed it, the prayer of the rower kneeling with the stroke of his oar, are true prayers heard throughout nature, though for cheap ends. Caratach, in Fletcher's "Bonduca," when admonished to inquire the mind of the god Audate, replies,—

"His hidden meaning lies in our endeavors;
Our valors are our best gods."

Another sort of false prayers are our regrets. Discontent is the want of self-reliance: it is infirmity of will. Regret calamities, if you can thereby help the sufferer; if not, attend your own work, and already the evil begins to be repaired. Our sympathy is just as base. We come to them who weep foolishly, and sit down and cry for company, instead of imparting to them truth and health in rough electric shocks, putting them once more in communication with their own reason. The secret of fortune is joy in our hands. Welcome evermore to gods and men is the self-helping man. For him all doors are flung wide: him all tongues greet, all honors crown, all eyes follow with desire. Our love goes out to him and embraces him, because he did not need it. We solicitously and apologetically caress and celebrate him, because he held on his way and scorned our disapprobation. The gods love him because men hated him. "To the persevering mortal," said Zoroaster, "the blessed Immortals are swift."

As men's prayers are a disease of the will, so are their creeds a disease of the intellect. They say with those foolish Israelites, 'Let not God speak to us, lest we die. Speak thou, speak any man with us, and we will obey.' Everywhere I am hindered of meeting God in my brother, because he has shut his own temple doors, and recites fables merely of his brother's, or his brother's brother's God. Every new mind is a new classification. If it prove a mind of uncommon activity and power, a Locke, a Lavoisier, a Hutton, a Bentham, a Fourier, it imposes its classification on other men, and lo! a new system. In proportion to the depth of the thought, and so to the number of the objects it touches and brings within reach of the pupil, is his complacency. But chiefly is this apparent in creeds and churches, which are also classifications of some powerful mind acting on the elemental thought of duty, and man's relation to the Highest. Such is Calvinism, Quakerism, Swedenborgism. The pupil takes the same delight in subordinating every thing to the new terminology, as a girl who has just learned botany in seeing a new earth and new seasons thereby. It will happen for a time, that the pupil will find his intellectual power has grown by the study of his master's mind. But in all unbalanced minds, the classification is idolized, passes for the end, and not for a speedily exhaustible means, so that the walls of the system blend to their eye in the remote horizon with the walls of the universe; the luminaries of heaven seem to them hung on the arch their master built. They cannot imagine how you aliens have any right to see,—how you can see; 'It must be somehow that you stole the light from us.' They do not yet perceive, that light, unsystematic, indomitable, will break into any cabin, even into theirs. Let them chirp awhile and call it their own. If they are honest and do well, presently their neat new pinfold will be too strait and low, will crack, will lean, will rot and vanish, and the immortal light, all young and joyful, million-orbed, million-colored, will beam over the universe as on the first morning.

2. It is for want of self-culture that the superstition of Traveling, whose idols are Italy, England, Egypt, retains its fascination for all educated Americans. They who made England, Italy, or Greece venerable in the imagination did so by sticking fast where they were, like an axis of the earth. In manly hours, we feel that duty is our place. The soul is no traveller; the wise man stays at home, and when his necessities, his duties, on any occasion call him from his house, or into foreign lands, he is at home still, and shall make men sensible by the expression of his countenance, that he goes the missionary of wisdom and virtue, and visits cities and men like a sovereign, and not like an interloper or a valet.

I have no churlish objection to the circumnavigation of the globe, for the purposes of art, of study, and benevolence, so that the man is first domesticated, or does not go abroad with the hope of finding somewhat greater than he knows. He who travels to be amused, or to get somewhat which he does not carry, travels away from himself, and grows old even in youth among old things. In Thebes, in Palmyra, his will and mind have become old and dilapidated as they. He carries ruins to ruins.

Traveling is a fool's paradise. Our first journeys discover to us the indifference of places. At home I dream that at Naples, at Rome, I can be intoxicated with beauty, and lose my sadness. I pack my trunk, embrace my friends, embark on the sea, and at last wake up in Naples, and there beside me is the stern fact, the sad self, unrelenting, identical, that I fled from. I seek the Vatican, and the palaces. I affect to be intoxicated with sights and suggestions, but I am not intoxicated. My giant goes with me wherever I go.

3. But the rage of traveling is a symptom of a deeper unsoundness affecting the whole intellectual action. The intellect is vagabond, and our system of education fosters restlessness. Our minds travel when our bodies are forced to stay at home. We imitate; and what is imitation but the traveling of the mind? Our houses are built with foreign taste; our shelves are garnished with foreign ornaments; our opinions, our tastes, our faculties, lean, and follow the Past and the Distant. The soul created the arts wherever they have flourished. It was in his own mind that the artist sought his model. It was an application of his own thought to the thing to be done and the conditions to be observed. And why need we copy the Doric or the Gothic model? Beauty, convenience, grandeur of thought, and quaint expression are as near to us as to any, and if the American artist will study with hope and love the precise thing to be done by him, considering the climate, the soil, the length of the day, the wants of the people, the habit and form of the government, he will create a house in which all these will find themselves fitted, and taste and sentiment will be satisfied also.

Insist on yourself; never imitate. Your own gift you can present every moment with the cumulative force of a whole life's cultivation; but of the adopted talent of another, you have only an extemporaneous, half possession. That which each can do best, none but his Maker can teach him. No man yet knows what it is, nor can, till that person has exhibited it. Where is the master who could have taught Shakespeare? Where is the master who could have instructed Franklin, or Washington, or Bacon, or Newton?

Every great man is a unique. The Scipionism of Scipio is precisely that part he could not borrow. Shakespeare will never be made by the study of Shakespeare. Do that which is assigned you, and you cannot hope too much or dare too much. There is at this moment for you an utterance brave and grand as that of the colossal chisel of Phidias, or trowel of the Egyptians, or the pen of Moses, or Dante, but different from all these. Not possibly will the soul all rich, all eloquent, with thousand-cloven tongue, deign to repeat itself; but if you can hear what these patriarchs say, surely you can reply to them in the same pitch of voice; for the ear and the tongue are two organs of one nature. Abide in the simple and noble regions of thy life, obey thy heart, and thou shalt reproduce the Foreworld again.

4. As our Religion, our Education, our Art look abroad, so does our spirit of society. All men plume themselves on the improvement of society, and no man improves.

Society never advances. It recedes as fast on one side as it gains on the other. It undergoes continual changes; it is barbarous, it is civilized, it is christianized, it is rich, it is scientific; but this change is not amelioration. For every thing that is given, something is taken. Society acquires new arts, and loses old instincts. What a contrast between the well-clad, reading, writing, thinking American, with a watch, a pencil, and a bill of exchange in his pocket, and the naked New Zealander, whose property is a club, a spear, a mat, and an undivided twentieth of a shed to sleep under! But compare the health of the two men, and you shall see that the white man has lost his aboriginal strength. If the traveller tell us truly, strike the savage with a broad axe, and in a day or two the flesh shall unite and heal as if you struck the blow into soft pitch, and the same blow shall send the white to his grave.

The civilized man has built a coach, but has lost the use of his feet. He is supported on crutches, but lacks so much support of muscle. He has a fine Geneva watch, but he fails of the skill to tell the hour by the sun. A Greenwich nautical almanac he has, and so being sure of the information when he wants it, the man in the street does not know a star in the sky. The solstice he does not observe; the equinox he knows as little; and the whole bright calendar of the year is without a dial in his mind. His note-books impair his memory; his libraries overload his wit; the insurance-office increases the number of accidents; and it may be a question whether machinery does not encumber; whether we have not lost by refinement some energy, by a Christianity entrenched in establishments and forms, some vigor of wild virtue. For every Stoic was a Stoic; but in Christendom where is the Christian?

There is no more deviation in the moral standard than in the standard of height or bulk. No greater men are now than ever were. A singular equality may be observed between the great men of the first and of the last ages; nor can all the science, art, religion, and philosophy of the nineteenth century avail to educate greater men than Plutarch's heroes, three or four and twenty centuries ago. Not in time is the race progressive. Phocion, Socrates, Anaxagoras, Diogenes, are great men, but they leave no class. He who is really of their class will not be called by their name, but will be his own man, and, in his turn, the founder of a sect. The arts and inventions of each period are only its costume, and do not invigorate men. The harm of the improved machinery may compensate its good. Hudson and Behring accomplished so much in their fishing-boats, as to astonish Parry and Franklin, whose equipment exhausted the resources of science and art. Galileo, with an opera-glass, discovered a more splendid series of celestial phenomena than any one since. Columbus found the New World in an undecked boat. It is curious to see the periodical disuse and perishing of means and machinery, which were introduced with loud laudation a few years or centuries before. The great genius returns to essential man. We reckoned the improvements of the art of war among the triumphs of science, and yet Napoleon conquered Europe by the bivouac, which consisted of falling back on naked valor, and disencumbering it of all aids. The Emperor held it impossible to make a perfect army, says Las Casas, "without abolishing our arms, magazines, commissaries, and carriages, until, in imitation of the Roman custom, the soldier should receive his supply of corn, grind it in his hand-mill, and bake his bread himself."

Society is a wave. The wave moves onward, but the water of which it is composed does not. The same particle does not rise from the valley to the ridge. Its unity is only phenomenal. The persons who make up a nation today, next year die, and their experience with them.

And so the reliance on Property, including the reliance on governments which protect it, is the want of self-reliance. Men have looked away from themselves and at things so long, that they have come to esteem the religious, learned, and civil institutions as guards of property, and they deprecate assaults on these, because they feel them to be assaults on property. They measure their esteem of each other by what each has, and not by what each is. But a cultivated man becomes ashamed of his property, out of new respect for his nature. Especially he hates what he has, if he see that it is accidental,—came to him by inheritance, or gift, or crime; then he feels that it is not having; it does not belong to him, has no root in him, and merely lies there, because no revolution or no robber takes it away. But that which a man is does always by necessity acquire, and what the man acquires is living property, which does not wait the beck of rulers, or mobs, or revolutions, or fire, or storm, or bankruptcies, but perpetually renews itself wherever the man breathes. "Thy lot or portion of life," said the Caliph Ali, "is seeking after thee; therefore be at rest from seeking after it." Our dependence on these foreign goods leads us to our slavish respect for numbers. The political parties meet in numerous conventions; the greater the concourse, and with each new uproar of announcement, The delegation from Essex! The Democrats from New Hampshire! The Whigs of Maine! the young patriot feels himself stronger than before by a new thousand of eyes and arms. In like manner the reformers summon conventions, and vote and resolve in multitude. Not so, O friends! will the God deign to enter and inhabit you, but by a method precisely the reverse. It is only as a man puts off all foreign support, and stands alone, that I see him to be strong and to prevail. He is weaker by every recruit to his banner. Is not a man better than a town? Ask nothing of men, and in the endless mutation, thou only firm column must presently appear the upholder of all that surrounds thee. He who knows that power is inborn, that he is weak because he has looked for good out of him and elsewhere, and so perceiving, throws himself unhesitatingly on his thought, instantly rights himself, stands in the erect position, commands his limbs, works miracles;

just as a man who stands on his feet is stronger than a man who stands on his head.

So use all that is called Fortune. Most men gamble with her, and gain all, and lose all, as her wheel rolls. But do thou leave as unlawful these winnings, and deal with Cause and Effect, the chancellors of God. In the Will work and acquire, and thou hast chained the wheel of Chance, and shalt sit hereafter out of fear from her rotations. A political victory, a rise of rents, the recovery of your sick, or the return of your absent friend, or some other favorable event, raises your spirits, and you think good days are preparing for you. Do not believe it. Nothing can bring you peace but yourself. Nothing can bring you peace but the triumph of principles.

Emerson's Keys to Success

Trust thyself: every heart vibrates to that iron string.

Whoso would be a man must be a nonconformist.

What I must do is all that concerns me, not what the people think.

Most men have bound their eyes with one or another handkerchief, and attached themselves to some one of these communities of opinion.

Live ever in a new day.

Speak what you think now in hard words, and tomorrow speak what tomorrow thinks in hard words again, though it contradict every thing you said today.

Greatness appeals to the future.

[A man] cannot be happy and strong until he lives with nature in the present, above time.

Nature suffers nothing to remain in her kingdoms which cannot help itself.

I must be myself.

With the exercise of self-trust, new powers shall appear.

Welcome evermore to gods and men is the self-helping man.

Insist on yourself; never imitate.

It is only as a man puts off all foreign support, and stands alone,

RALPH WALDO EMERSON

Greatness

There is a prize which we are all aiming at, and the more power and goodness we have, so much more the energy of that aim. Every human being has a right to it, and in the pursuit we do not stand in each other's way. For it has a long scale of degrees, a wide variety of views, and every aspirant, by his success in the pursuit, does not hinder but helps his competitors. I might call it completeness, but that is later,—perhaps adjourned for ages. I prefer to call it Greatness. It is the fulfillment of a natural tendency in each man. It is a fruitful study. It is the best tonic to the young soul. And no man is unrelated; therefore we admire eminent men, not for themselves, but as representatives. It is very certain that we ought not to be and shall not be contented with any goal we have reached. Our aim is no less than greatness; that which invites all, belongs to us all, to which we are all sometimes untrue, cowardly, faithless, but of which we never quite despair, and which, in every sane moment, we resolve to make our own. It is also the only platform on which all men can meet. What anecdotes of any man do we wish to hear or read? Only the best. Certainly not those in which he was degraded to the level of dulness or vice, but those in which he rose above all competition by obeying a light that shone to him alone. This is the worthiest history of the world.

Greatness,—what is it? Is there not some injury to us, some insult in the word? What we commonly call greatness is only such in our barbarous or infant experience. 'Tis not the soldier, not Alexander or Bonaparte or

Count Moltke surely, who represent the highest force of mankind; not the strong hand, but wisdom and civility, the creation of laws, institutions, letters and art. These we call by distinction the humanities; these, and not the strong arm and brave heart, which are also indispensable to their defense. For the scholars represent the intellect, by which man is man; the intellect and the moral sentiment,—which in the last analysis can never be separated. Who can doubt the potency of an individual mind, who sees the shock given to torpid races—torpid for ages—by Mahornet; a vibration propagated over Asia and Africa? What of Menu? What of Buddha? of Shakespeare? of Newton? of Franklin?

There are certain points of identity in which these masters agree. Self-respect is the early form in which greatness appears. The man in the tavern maintains his opinion, though the whole crowd takes the other side; we are at once drawn to him. The porter or truckman refuses a reward for finding your purse, or for pulling you drowning out of the river. Thereby, with the service, you have got a moral lift. You say of some new person, That man will go far,—for you see in his manners that the recognition of him by others is not necessary to him. And what a bittersweet sensation when we have gone to pour out our acknowledgment of a man's nobleness, and found him quite indifferent to our good opinion! They may well fear Fate who have any infirmity of habit or aim; but he who rests on what he is, has a destiny above destiny, and can make mouths at Fortune. If a man's centrality is incomprehensible to us, we may as well snub the sun. There is something in Archimedes or in Luther or Samuel Johnson that needs no protection. There is somewhat in the true scholar which he cannot be laughed out of, nor be terrified or bought off from. Stick to your own; don't inculpate yourself in the local, social or national crime, but follow the path your genius traces like the galaxy of heaven for you to walk in.

A sensible person will soon see the folly and wickedness of thinking to please. Sensible men are very rare. A sensible man does not brag, avoids introducing the names of his creditable companions, omits himself as habitually as another man obtrudes himself in the discourse, and is content with putting his fact or theme simply on its ground. You shall not tell me that your commercial house, your partners or yourself are of importance; you shall not tell me that you have learned to know men; you shall make me feel that; your saying so unsays it. You shall not enumerate your brilliant acquaintances, nor tell me by their titles what books you have read. I am to infer that you keep good company by your better information and manners, and to infer your reading from the wealth and accuracy of your conversation.

Young men think that the manly character requires that they should go to California, or to India, or into the army. When they have learned that the parlor and the college and the counting-room demand as much courage as the sea or the camp, they will be willing to consult their own strength and education in their choice of place.

There are to each function and department of Nature supplementary men: to geology, sinewy, out-of-doors men, with a taste for mountains and rocks, a quick eye for differences and for chemical changes. Give such, first a course in chemistry, and then a geological survey. Others find a charm and a profession in the natural history of man and the mammalian or related animals; others in ornithology, or fishes, or insects; others in plants; others in the elements of which the whole world is made. These lately have stimulus to their study through the extraordinary revelations of the spectroscope that the sun and the planets are made in part or in whole of the same elements as the earth is. Then there is the boy who is born with a taste for the sea, and must go thither if he has to run away from his father's house to the forecastle; another longs for travel in foreign lands; another will be a lawyer; another, an astronomer; an other, a painter, sculptor, architect or engineer. Thus there is not a piece of Nature in any kind but a man is born, who, as his genius opens, aims slower or faster to dedicate himself to that. Then there is the poet, the philosopher, the politician, the orator, the clergyman, the physician. 'Tis gratifying to see this adaptation of man to the world, and to every part and particle of it.

Many readers remember that Sir Humphry Davy said, when he was praised for his important discoveries, "My best discovery was Michael Faraday." In 1848 I had the privilege of hearing Professor Faraday deliver, in the Royal Institution in London, a lecture on what he called Diamagnetism,—by which he meant cross-magnetism; and he showed us various experiments on certain gases, to prove that whilst ordinarily magnetism of steel is from north to south, in other substances, gases, it acts from east to west. And further experiments led him to the theory that every chemical substance would be found to have its own, and a different, polarity. I do not know how far his experiments and others have been pushed in this matter, but one fact is clear to me, that diamagnetism is a law of the mind, to the full extent of Faraday's idea; namely, that every mind has a new compass, a new north, a new direction of its own, differencing its genius and aim from every other mind; as every man, with whatever family re semblances, has a new countenance, new manner, new voice, new thoughts and new character. Whilst he shares with all mankind the gift of reason and the moral sentiment, there is a teaching for him from within which is leading him in a new path, and, the more it is trusted, separates and signalizes him, while it makes him more important and necessary to society. We call this specialty the bias of each individual. And none of us will ever accomplish any thing excellent or commanding except when he listens to this whisper which is heard by him alone. Swedenborg called it the *pro prium*,—not a thought shared with others, but constitutional to the man. A point of education that I can never too much insist upon is this tenet that every individual man has a bias which he must obey, and that it is only as he feels and obeys this that he rightly develops and attains his legitimate power in the world. It is his magnetic needle, which points always in one direction to his proper path, with more or less variation from any other man's. He is never happy nor strong until he finds it, keeps it; learns to be at home with himself; learns to watch the delicate hints and insights that come to him, and to have the entire assurance of his own mind. And in this self-respect or hearkening to the privatest oracle, he consults his ease, I may say, or need never be at a loss. In morals this is conscience; in intellect, genius; in practice, talent;—not to imitate or surpass a particular man in his way, but to bring out your own new way; to each his own method, style, wit, eloquence. It is easy for a commander to command. Clinging to Nature, or to that province of Nature which he knows, he makes no mistakes, but works after her laws and at her own pace, so that his doing, which is perfectly natural, appears miraculous to dull people. Montluc, the great marshal of France, says of the Genoese admiral, Andrew Doria, "It seemed as if the sea stood in awe of this man." And a kindred genius, Nelson, said, "I feel that I am fitter to do the action than to describe it." Therefore I will say that another trait of greatness is facility.

This necessity of resting on the real, of speaking your private thought and experience, few young men apprehend. Set ten men to write their journal for one day, and nine of them will leave out their thought, or proper result, that is, their net experience,—and lose themselves in misreporting the supposed experience of other people. Indeed I think it an essential caution to young writers, that they shall not in their discourse leave out the one thing which the discourse was written to say. Let that belief which you hold alone, have free course. I have observed that in all public speaking, the rule of the orator begins, not in the array of his facts, but when his deep conviction, and the right and necessity he feels to convey that conviction to his audience,—when these shine and burn in his address; when the thought which he stands for gives its own authority to him, adds to him a grander personality, gives him valor, breadth and new intellectual power, so that not he, but mankind, seems to speak through his lips. There is a certain transfiguration; all great orators have it, and men who wish to be orators simulate it.

If we should ask ourselves what is this self-respect, it would carry us to the highest problems. It is our practical perception of the Deity in man. It has its deep foundations in religion. If you have ever known a good mind among the Quakers, you will have found that is the element of their faith. As they express it, it might be thus: "I do not pretend to any commandment or large revelation, but if at any time I form some plan, propose a journey or a course of conduct, I perhaps find a silent obstacle in my mind that I cannot account for. Very well,—I let it lie, thinking it may pass away, but if it do not pass away I yield to it, obey it. You ask me to describe it. I cannot describe it. It is not an oracle, nor an angel, nor a dream, nor a law; it is too simple to be described, it is but a grain of mustard-seed, but such as it is, it is something which the contradiction of all mankind could not shake, and which the consent of all mankind could not confirm."

You are rightly fond of certain books or men that you have found to excite your reverence and emulation. But none of these can compare with the greatness of that counsel which is open to you in happy solitude. I mean that there is for you the following of an inward leader,—a slow discrimination that there is for each a Best Counsel which enjoins the fit word and the fit act for every moment. And the path of each, pursued, leads to greatness. How grateful to find in man or woman a new emphasis of their own.

But if the first rule is to obey your native bias, to accept that work for which you were inwardly formed,—the second rule is concentration, which doubles its force. Thus if you are a scholar, be that. The same laws hold for you as for the laborer. The shoemaker makes a good shoe because he makes nothing else. Let the student mind his own charge; sedulously wait every morning for the news concerning the structure of the world which the spirit will give him.

No way has been found for making heroism easy, even for the scholar. Labor, iron labor, is for him. The world was created as an audience for him; the atoms of which it is made are opportunities. Read the performance of Bentley, of Gibbon, of Cuvier, Geoffroy Saint-Hilaire, Laplace. "He can toil terribly," said Cecil of Sir Walter Raleigh. These few words sting and bite and lash us when we are frivolous. Let us get out of the way of their blows by making them true of ourselves. There is so much to be done that we ought to begin quickly to bestir ourselves. This day-labor of ours, we confess, has hitherto a certain emblematic air, like the annual ploughing and sewing of the Emperor of China. Let us make it an honest sweat. Let the scholar measure his valor by his power to cope with intellectual giants. Leave others to count votes and calculate stocks. His courage is to weigh Plato, judge Laplace, know Newton, Faraday, judge of Darwin, criticize Kant and Swedenborg, and on all these arouse the central courage of insight. The scholar's courage should be as terrible as the Cid's, though it grow out of spiritual nature, not out of brawn. Nature, when she adds difficulty, adds brain.

With this respect to the bias of the individual mind add, what is consistent with it, the most catholic receptivity for the genius of others. The day will come when no badge, uniform or medal will be worn; when the eye, which carries in it planetary influences from all the stars, will indicate rank fast enough by exerting power. For it is true that the stratification of crusts in geology is not more precise than the degrees of rank in minds. A man will say: "I am born to this position; I must take it, and neither you nor I can help or hinder me. Surely, then, I need not fret myself to guard my own dignity." The great man loves the conversation or the book that convicts him, not that which soothes or flatters him. He makes himself of no reputation; he conceals his learning, conceals his charity. For the highest wisdom does not concern itself with particular men, but with man enamored with the law and the Eternal Source. Say with Antoninus, "If the picture is good, who cares who made it? What matters it by whom the good is done, by yourself or an other?" If it is the truth, what matters who said it? If it was right, what signifies who did it? All greatness is in degree, and there is more above than below. Where were your own intellect, if greater had not lived? And do you know what the right meaning of Fame is? It is that sympathy, rather that fine element by which the good become partners of the greatness of their superiors.

Extremes meet, and there is no better example than the haughtiness of humility. No aristocrat, no prince born to the purple, can begin to compare with the self-respect of the saint. Why is he so lowly, but that he knows that he can well afford it, resting on the largeness of God in him? I have read in an old book that Barcena the Jesuit confessed to another of his order that when the Devil appeared to him in his cell one night, out of his profound humility he rose up to meet him, and prayed him to sit down in his chair, for he was more worthy to sit there than himself.

Shall I tell you the secret of the true scholar? It is this: Every man I meet is my master in some point, and in that I learn of him. The .populace will say, with Horne Tooke, "If you would be powerful, pretend to be powerful." I prefer to say, with the old Hebrew prophet, "Seekest thou great things? seek them not;" or, what was said of the Spanish prince, "The more you took from him, the greater he appeared," *Plus on lui ote, plus it est grand.*

Scintillations of greatness appear here and there in men of unequal character, and arc by no means confined to the cultivated and so-called moral class. It is easy to draw traits from Napoleon, who was not generous nor just, but was intellectual and knew the law of things. Napoleon commands our respect by his enormous self-trust, the habit of seeing with his own eyes, never the surface, but to the heart of the matter, whether it was a road, a cannon, a character, an officer, or a king,—and by the speed and security of his action in the premises, always new. He has left a library of manuscripts, a multitude of sayings, every one of widest application. He was a man who always fell on his feet. When one of his favorite schemes missed, he had the faculty of taking up his genius, as he said, and of carrying it somewhere else. "Whatever they may tell you, believe that one fights with cannon as with fists; when once the fire is begun, the least want of ammunition renders what you have done already useless." I find it easy to translate all his technics into all of mine, and his official advices are to me more literary and philosophical than the memoirs of the Academy. His advice to his brother, King Joseph of Spain, was: "I have only one counsel for you,—Be Master." Depth of intellect relieves even the ink of crime with a fringe of light. We perhaps look on its crimes as experiments of a universal student; as he may read any book who reads all books, and as the English judge in old times, when learning was rare, forgave a culprit who could read and write. It is difficult to find greatness pure. Well, I please myself with its diffusion; to find a spark of true fire amid much corruption. It is some guaranty. I hope, for the health of the soul which has this generous blood. How many men, detested in contemporary hostile history, of whom, now that the mists have rolled away, we have learned to correct our old estimates, and to see them as, on the whole, instruments of great benefit. Diderot was no model, but unclean as the society in which he lived; yet was he the best-natured man in France, and would help any wretch at a pinch. His humanity knew no bounds. A poor scribbler who had written a lampoon against him and wished to dedicate it to a pious Duc d'Orleans, came with it in his poverty to Diderot, and Diderot, pitying the creature, wrote the dedication for him, and so raised five-and-twenty louis to save his famishing lampooner alive.

Meantime we hate sniveling. I do not wish you to surpass others in any narrow or professional or monkish way. We like the natural greatness of health and wild power. I confess that I am as much taken by it in boys, and sometimes in people not normal, nor educated, nor presentable, nor church-members,—even in persons open to the suspicion of irregular and immoral living, in Bohemians,—as in more orderly examples. For we must remember that [in the lives of soldiers, sailors and men of large adventure, many of the stays and guards of our household life are wanting, and yet the opportunities and incentives to sublime daring and performance are often close at hand. We must have some charity for the sense of the people, which admires natural power, and will elect it over virtuous men who have less. It has this excuse, that natural is really allied to moral power, and may always be expected to approach it by its own instincts. Intellect at least is not stupid, and will see the force of morals over men, if it does not itself obey. Henry VII. of England was a wise king. When Gerald, Earl of Kildare, who was in rebellion against him, was brought to London, and examined before the Privy Council, one said, "All Ireland cannot govern this Earl." "Then let this Earl govern all Ireland," replied the King.

It is noted of some scholars, like Swift and Gibbon and Donne, that they pretended to vices which they had not, so much did they hate hypocrisy. William Blake the artist frankly says, "I never knew a bad man in whom there was not something very good." Bret Harte has pleased himself with noting and recording the sudden virtue blazing in the wild reprobates of the ranches and mines of California.

Men are ennobled by morals and by intellect; but those two elements know each other and always beckon to each other, until at last they meet in the man, if he is to be truly great. The man who sells you a lamp shows you that the flame of oil, which contented you before, casts a strong shade in the path of the petroleum which he lights behind it; and this again casts a shadow in the path of the electric light. So does intellect when brought into the presence of character; character puts out that light. Goethe, in his correspondence with his Grand Duke of Weimar, does not shine. We can see that the Prince had the advantage of the Olympian genius. It is more plainly seen in the correspondence between Voltaire and Frederick of Prussia. Voltaire is brilliant, nimble and various, but Frederick has the superior tone. But it is curious that Byron writes down to Scott; Scott writes up to him. The Greeks surpass all men till they face the Romans, when Roman character prevails over Greek genius. Whilst degrees of intellect interest only classes of men who pursue the same studies, as chemists or astronomers, mathematicians or linguists, and have no attraction for the crowd, there are always men who have a more catholic genius, are really great as men, and inspire universal enthusiasm. A great style of hero draws equally all classes, all the extremes of society, till we say the very dogs believe in him. We have had such examples in this country, in Daniel Webster, Henry Clay, and the seamen's preacher, Father Taylor; in England, Charles James Fox; in Scotland, Robert Burns; and in France, though it is less intelligible to us, Voltaire. Abraham Lincoln is perhaps the most remarkable example of this class that we have seen,—a man who was at home and welcome with the humblest, and with a spirit and a practical vein in the times of terror that commanded the admiration of the wisest. His heart was as great as the world, but there was no room in it to hold the memory of a wrong.

These may serve as local examples to indicate a magnetism which is probably known better and finer to each scholar in the little Olympus of his own favorites, and which makes him require geniality and humanity in his heroes. What are these but the promise and the preparation of a day when the air of the world shall be purified by nobler society, when the measure of greatness shall be usefulness in the highest sense, greatness consisting in truth, reverence and good will?

Life is made of illusions, and a very common one is the opinion you hear expressed in every village: "O yes, if I lived in New York or Philadelphia, Cambridge or New Haven or Boston or Andover, there might be fit society; but it happens that there are no fine young men, no superior women in my town." You may hear this every day; but it is a shallow remark. Ah! have you yet to learn that the eye altering alters all; that "the world is an echo which returns to each of us what we say"? It is not examples of greatness, but sensibility to see them, that is wanting. The good botanist will find flowers between the street pavements, and any man filled with an idea or a purpose will find examples and illustrations and coadjutors wherever he goes. Wit is a magnet to find wit, and character to find character. Do you not know that people are as those with whom they converse? And if all or any are heavy to me, that fact accuses me. Why complain, as if a man's debt to his inferiors were not at least equal to his debt to his superiors? If men were equals, the waters would not move; but the difference of level which makes Niagara a cataract, makes eloquence, indignation, poetry, in him who finds there is much to communicate. With self-respect then there must be in the aspirant the strong fellow feeling, the humanity, which makes men of all classes warm to him as their leader and representative.

We are thus forced to express our instinct of the truth by exposing the failures of experience. The man whom we have not seen, in whom no regard of self degraded the adorer of the laws,—who by governing himself governed others; sportive in manner, but inexorable in act; who sees longevity in his cause; whose aim is always distinct to him; who is suffered to be himself in society; who carries fate in his eye;—he it is whom we seek, encouraged in every good hour that here or hereafter he shall be found.

Emerson's Keys to Success

Stick to your own; follow the path your genius traces like the galaxy of heaven for you to walk in.

None of us will ever accomplish any thing excellent or commanding except when he listens to this whisper which is heard by him alone.

If the first rule is to obey your native bias, to accept that work for which you were inwardly formed,— the second rule is concentration, which doubles its force.

"The world is an echo which returns to each of us what we say."

Courage

So nigh is grandeur to our dust,
So near is God to man,
When Duty whispers low, Thou must,
The youth replies, I can.

Peril around, all else appalling,
Cannon in front and leaden rain,
Him duty, through the clarion calling
To the van, called not in vain.

I observe that there are three qualities which conspicuously attract the wonder and reverence of mankind:

1. Disinterestedness, as shown in indifference to the ordinary bribes and influences of conduct,—a purpose so sincere and generous that it cannot be tempted aside by any prospects of wealth or other private advantage. Self-love is, in almost all men, such an over-weight, that they are incredulous of a man's habitual preference of the general good to his own; but when they see it proved by sacrifices of ease, wealth, rank, and of life itself, there is no limit to their admiration. This has made the power of the saints of the East and West, who have led the religion of great nations. Self-sacrifice is the real miracle out of which all the reported miracles grew.

This makes the renown of the heroes of Greece and Rome,—of Socrates, Aristides and Phocion; of Quintus Curtius, Cato and Regulu; of Hatem Tai's hospitality; of Chatham, whose scornful magnanimity gave him immense popularity; of Washington, giving his service to the public without salary or reward.

2. Practical power. Men admire the man who can organize their wishes and thoughts in stone and wood and steel and brass,—the man who can build the boat, who has the impiety to make the rivers run the way he wants them; who can lead his telegraph through the ocean from shore to shore; who, sitting in his closet, can lay out the plans of a campaign, sea-war and land-war, such that the best generals and admirals, when all is done, see that they must thank him for success; the power of better combination and foresight, however exhibited, whether it only plays a game of chess, or whether, more loftily, a cunning mathematician, penetrating the cubic weights of stars, predicts the planet which eyes had never seen; or whether, exploring the chemical elements whereof we and the world are made, and seeing their secret, Franklin draws off the lightning in his hand; suggesting that one day a wiser geology shall make the earthquake harmless and the volcano an agricultural resource. Or here is one who, seeing the wishes of men, knows how to come at their end; whispers to this friend, argues down that adversary, moulds society to his purpose, and looks at all men as wax for his hands; takes command of them as the wind does of clouds, as the mother does of the child, or the man that knows more does of the man that knows less, and leads them in glad surprise to the very point where they would be: this man is followed with acclamation.

3. The third excellence is courage, the perfect will, which no terrors can shake, which is attracted by frowns or threats or hostile armies, nay, needs these to awake and fan its reserved energies into a pure flame, and is never quite itself until the hazard is extreme; then it is serene and fertile, and all its powers play well. There is a Hercules, an Achilles, a Rustem, an Arthur or a Cid in the mythology of every nation; and in authentic history, a Leonidas, a Scipio, a Caesar, a Richard Coeur de Lion, a Cromwell, a

Nelson, a Great Conde, a Bertrand du Guesclin, a Doge Dandolo, a Napoleon, a Massaena, and Ney. 'Tis said courage is common, but the immense esteem in which it is held proves it to be rare. Animal resistance, the instinct of the male animal when cornered, is no doubt common; but the pure article, courage with eyes, courage with conduct, self-possession at the cannon's mouth, cheerfulness in lonely adherence to the right, is the endowment of elevated characters. I need not show how much it is esteemed, for the people give it the first rank. They forgive everything to it. What an ado we make through two thousand years about Thermopylae and Salamis! What a memory of Poitiers and Crecy, and Bunker Hill, and Washington's endurance! And any man who puts his life in peril in a cause which is esteemed becomes the darling of all men. The very nursery-books, the ballads which delight boys, the romances which delight men, the favorite topics of eloquence, the thunderous emphasis which orators give to every martial defiance and passage of arms, and which the people greet, may testify. How short a time since this whole nation rose every morning to read or to hear the traits of courage of its sons and brothers in the field, and was never weary of the theme! We have had examples of men who, for showing effective courage on a single occasion, have become a favorite spectacle to nations, and must be brought in chariots to every mass meeting.

Men are so charmed with valor that they have pleased themselves with being called lions, leopards, eagles and dragons, from the animals contemporary with us in the geologic formations. But the animals have great advantage of us in precocity. Touch the snapping-turtle with a stick, and he seizes it with his teeth. Cut off his head, and the teeth will not let go the stick. Break the egg of the young, and the little embryo, before yet the eyes are open, bites fiercely; these vivacious creatures contriving—shall we say?— not only to bite after they are dead, but also to bite before they are born.

But man begins life helpless. The babe is in paroxysms of fear the moment its nurse leaves it alone, and it comes so slowly to any power of self-protection that mothers say the salvation of the life and health of a young child is a perpetual miracle. The terrors of the child are quite reasonable, and add to his loveliness; for his utter ignorance and weakness, and his enchanting indignation on such a small basis of capital compel every by-stander to take his part. Every moment as long as he is awake he studies the use of his eyes, ears, hands and feet, learning how to meet and avoid his dangers, and thus every hour loses one terror more. But this education stops too soon. A large majority of men being bred in families and beginning early to be occupied day by day with some routine of safe industry, never come to the rough experiences that make the Indian, the soldier or the frontiersman self-subsistent and fearless. Hence the high price of courage indicates the general timidity. "Mankind," said Franklin, "are dastardly when they meet with opposition." In war even generals are seldom found eager to give battle. Lord Wellington said, "Uniforms were often masks; "and again, "When my journal appears, many statues must come down." The Norse Sagas relate that when Bishop Magne reproved King Sigurd for his wicked divorce, the priest who attended the bishop, expecting every moment when the savage king would burst with rage and slay his superior, said that he "saw the sky no bigger than a calf-skin." And I remember when a pair of Irish girls who had been run away with in a wagon by a skittish horse, said that when he began to rear, they were so frightened that they could not see the horse.

Cowardice shuts the eyes till the sky is not larger than a calf-skin; shuts the eyes so that we cannot see the horse that is running away with us; worse, shuts the eyes of the mind and chills the heart. Fear is cruel and mean. The political reigns of terror have been reigns of madness and malignity, a total perversion of opinion; society is upside down, and its best men are thought too bad to live. Then the protection which a house, a family, neighborhood and property, even the first accumulation of savings gives, go in all times to generate this taint of the respectable classes. Those political parties which gather in the well-disposed portion of the community,—how infirm and ignoble! what white lips they have! always on the defensive, as if the lead were entrusted to the journals, often written in great part by women and boys, who, without strength, wish to keep up the appearance of strength. They can do the hurrahs, the placarding, the flags,— and the voting, if it is a fair day; but the aggressive attitude of men who will have right done, will no longer be bothered with burglars and ruffians in the streets, counterfeiters in public offices, and thieves on the bench; that part, the part of the leader and soul of the vigilance committee, must be taken by stout and sincere men who are really angry and determined. In ordinary, we have a snappish criticism which watches and contradicts the opposite party. We want the will which advances and dictates. When we get an advantage, as in Congress the other day, it is because our adversary has committed a fault, not that we have taken the initiative and given the law. Nature has made up her mind that what cannot defend itself shall not be defended. Complaining never so loud and with never so much reason is of no use. One heard much cant of peace-parties long ago in Kansas and elsewhere, that their strength lay in the greatness of their wrongs, and dissuading all resistance, as if to make this strength greater. But were their wrongs greater than the negro's? And what kind of strength did they ever give him? It was always invitation to the tyrant, and bred disgust in those who would protect the victim. What cannot stand must fall; and the measure of our sincerity and therefore of the respect of men, is the amount of health and wealth we will hazard in the defense of our right. An old farmer, my neighbor across the fence, when I ask him if he is not going to town-meeting, says: "No; 'tis no use balloting, for it will not stay; but what you do with the gun will stay so.'" Nature has charged every one with his own defense as with his own support, and the only title I can have to your help is when I have manfully put forth all the means I possess to keep me, and being overborne by odds, the by-standers have a natural wish to interfere and see fair play.

But with this pacific education we have no readiness for bad times. I am much mistaken if every man who went to the army in the late war had not a lively curiosity to know how he should behave in action. Tender, amiable boys, who had never encountered any rougher play than a baseball match or a fishing excursion, were suddenly drawn up to face a bayonet charge or capture a battery. Of course they must each go into that action with a certain despair. Each whispers to himself: "My exertions must be of small account to the result; only will the benignant Heaven save me from disgracing myself and my friends and my State. Die! O yes, I can well die; but I cannot afford to misbehave; and I do not know how I shall feel." So great a soldier as the old French Marshal Montluc acknowledges that he has often trembled with fear, and recovered courage when he had said a prayer for the occasion. I knew a young soldier who died in the early campaign, who confided to his sister that he had made up his mind to volunteer for the war. "I have not," he said, "any proper courage, but I shall never let any one find it out." And he had accustomed himself always to go into whatever place of danger, and do whatever he was afraid to do, setting a dogged resolution to resist this natural infirmity. Coleridge has preserved an anecdote of an officer in the British Navy who told him that when he, in his first boat expedition, a midshipman in his fourteenth year, accompanied Sir Alexander Ball, as we were rowing up to the vessel we were to attack, amid a discharge of musketry, I was overpowered with fear, my knees shook and I was ready to faint away. Lieutenant Ball seeing me, placed himself close beside me, took hold of my hand and whispered, 'Courage, my dear boy! you will recover in a minute or so; I was just the same when I first went out in this way.' It was as if an angel spoke to me. From that moment I was as fearless and as forward as the oldest of the boat's crew. But I dare not think what would have become of me, if, at that moment, he had scoffed and exposed me."

Knowledge is the antidote to fear,—Knowledge, Use and Reason, with its higher aids. The child is as much in danger from a staircase, or the firegrate, or a bathtub, or a cat, as the soldier from a cannon or an ambush. Each surmounts the fear as fast as he precisely understands the peril and learns the means of resistance. Each is liable to panic, which is, exactly, the terror of ignorance surrendered to the imagination. Knowledge is the encourager, knowledge that takes fear out of the heart, know-ledge and use, which is knowledge in practice. They can conquer who believe they can. It is he who has done the deed once who does not shrink from attempting it again. It is the groom who knows the jumping horse well who can safely ride him. It is the veteran soldier, who, seeing the flash of the cannon, can step aside from the path of the ball. Use makes a better soldier than the most urgent considerations of duty,—familiarity with danger enabling him to estimate the danger. He sees how much is the risk, and is not afflicted with imagination; knows practically Marshal Saxe's rule, that every soldier killed costs the enemy his weight in lead.

The sailor loses fear as fast as he acquires command of sails and spars and steam; the frontiersman, when he has a perfect rifle and has acquired a sure aim. To the sailor's experience every new circumstance suggests what he must do. The terrific chances which make the hours and the minutes long to the passenger, he whiles away by incessant application of expedients and repairs. To him a leak, a hurricane, or a water-spout is so much work,—no more. The hunter is not alarmed by bears, catamounts or wolves, nor the grazier by his bull, nor the dog-breeder by his bloodhound, nor an Arab by the simoon, nor a farmer by a fire in the woods. The forest on fire looks discouraging enough to a citizen: the farmer is skillful to fight it. The neighbors run together; with pine boughs they can mop out the flame, and by raking with the hoe a long but little trench, confine to a patch the fire which would easily spread over a hundred acres.

In short, courage consists in equality to the problem before us. The school-boy is daunted before his tutor by a question of arithmetic, because he does not yet command the simple steps of the solution which the boy beside him has mastered. These once seen, he is as cool as Archimedes, and cheerily proceeds a step farther. Courage is equality to the problem, in affairs, in science, in trade, in council, or in action; consists in the conviction that the agents with whom you contend are not superior in strength of resources or spirit to you. The general must stimulate the mind of his soldiers to the perception that they are men, and the enemy is no more. Knowledge, yes; for the danger of dangers is illusion. The eye is easily daunted; and the drums, flags, shining helmets, beard and mustache of the soldier have conquered you long before his sword or bayonet reaches you.

But we do not exhaust the subject in the slight analysis; we must not forget the variety of temperaments, each of which qualifies this power of resistance. It is observed that men with little imagination are less fearful; they wait till they feel pain, whilst others of more sensibility anticipate it, and suffer in the fear of the pang more acutely than in the pang. 'Tis certain that the threat is sometimes more formidable than the stroke, and 'tis possible that the beholders suffer more keenly than the victims. Bodily pain is superficial, seated usually in the skin and the extremities, for the sake of giving us warning to put us on our guard; not in the vitals, where the rupture that produces death is perhaps not felt, and the victim never knew what hurt him. Pain is superficial, and therefore fear is. The torments of martyrdoms are probably most keenly felt by the by-standers. The torments are illusory. The first suffering is the last suffering, the later hurts being lost on insensibility. Our affections and wishes for the external welfare of the hero tumultuously rush to expression in tears and outcries: but we, like him, subside into indifferency and defiance when we perceive how short is the longest arm of malice, how serene is the sufferer.

It is plain that there is no separate essence called courage, no cup or cell in the brain, no vessel in the heart containing drops or atoms that make or give this virtue; but it is the right or healthy state of every man, when he is free to do that which is constitutional to him to do. It is directness, —the instant performing of that which he ought. The thoughtful man says, You differ from me in opinion and methods, but do you not see that I cannot think or act otherwise than I do? that my way of living is organic? And to be really strong we must adhere to our own means. On organic action all strength depends. Hear what women say of doing a task by sheer force of will: it costs them a fit of sickness. Plutarch relates that the Pythoness who tried to prophesy without command in the Temple at Delphi, though she performed the usual rites, and inhaled the air of the cavern standing on the tripod, fell into convulsions and died. Undoubtedly there is a temperamental courage, a warlike blood, which loves a fight, does not feel itself except in a quarrel, as one sees in wasps, or ants, or cocks, or cats. The like vein appears in certain races of men and in individuals of every race. I n every school there are certain fighting boys; in every society, the contradicting men; in every town, bravoes and bullies, better or worse dressed, fancy-men, patrons of the cock-pit and the ring. Courage is temperamental, scientific, ideal. Swedenborg has left this record of his king: "Charles XII of Sweden did not know what that was which others called fear, nor what that spurious valor and daring that is excited by inebriating draughts, for he never tasted any liquid but pure water. Of him we may say that he led a life more remote from death, and in fact lived more, than any other man." It was told of the Prince of Conde that "there not being a more furious man in the world, danger in fight never disturbs him more than just to make him civil, and to command in words of great obligation to his officers and men, and without any the least disturbance to his judgment or spirit." Each has his own courage, as his own talent; but the courage of the tiger is one, and of the horse another. The dog that scorns to fight, will fight for his master. The llama that will carry a load if you caress him, will refuse food and die if he is scourged. The fury of onset is one, and of calm endurance another. There is a courage of the cabinet as well as a courage of the field; a courage of manners in private assemblies, and another in public assemblies; a courage which enables one man to speak masterly to a hostile company, whilst another man who can easily face a cannon's mouth dares not open his own.

There is a courage of a merchant in dealing with his trade, by which dangerous turns of affairs are met and prevailed over. Merchants recognize as much gallantry, well judged too, in the conduct of a wise and upright man of business in difficult times, as soldiers in a soldier.

There is a courage in the treatment of every art by a master in architecture, in sculpture, in painting or in poetry, each cheering the mind of the spectator or receiver as by true strokes of genius, which yet nowise implies the presence of physical valor in the artist. This is the courage of genius, in every kind. A certain quantity of power belongs to a certain quantity of faculty. The beautiful voice at church goes sounding on, and covers up in its volume, as in a cloak, all the defects of the choir. The singers, I observe, all yield to it, and so the fair singer indulges her instinct, and dares, and dares, because she knows she can.

It gives the cutting edge to every profession. The judge puts his mind to the tangle of contradictions in the case, squarely accosts the question, and by not being afraid of it, by dealing with it as business which must be disposed of, he sees presently that common arithmetic and common methods apply to this affair. Perseverance strips it of all peculiarity, and ranges it on the same ground as other business. Morphy played a daring game in chess: the daring was only an illusion of the spectator, for the player sees his move to be well fortified and safe. You may see the same dealing in criticism; a new book astonishes for a few days, takes itself out of common jurisdiction, and nobody knows what to say of it: but the scholar is not deceived. The old principles which books exist to express are more beautiful than any book; and out of love of the reality he is an expert judge how far the book has approached it and where it has come short. In all applications it is the same power,—the habit of reference to one's own mind, as the home of all truth and counsel, and which can easily dispose of any book because it can very well do without all books. When a confident man comes into a company magnifying this or that author he has freshly read, the company grow silent and ashamed of their ignorance. But I remember the old professor, whose searching mind engraved every word he spoke on the memory of the class, when we asked if he had read this or that shining novelty, "No, I have never read that book;" instantly the book lost credit, and was not to be heard of again

Every creature has a courage of his constitution fit for his duties: Archimedes, the courage of a geometer to stick to his diagram, heedless of the siege and sack of the city; and the Roman soldier his faculty to strike at Archimedes. Each is strong, relying on his own, and each is betrayed when he seeks in himself the courage of others.

Captain John Brown, the hero of Kansas, said to me in conversation, that "for a settler in a new country, one good, believing, strong-minded man is worth a hundred, nay, a thousand men without character; and that the right men will give a permanent direction to the fortunes of a state. As for the bullying drunkards of which armies are usually made up, he thought cholera, small-pox and consumption as valuable recruits." He held the belief that courage and chastity are silent concerning themselves. He said, "As soon as I hear one of my men say, 'Ah, let me only get my eye on such a man, I'll bring him down,' I don't expect much aid in the fight from that talker. 'Tis the quiet, peaceable men, the men of principle, that make the best soldiers."

" 'Tis still observed those men most valiant are Who are most modest ere they came to war."

True courage is not ostentatious; men who wish to inspire terror seem thereby to confess themselves cowards. Why do they rely on it, but because they know how potent it is with themselves?

The true temper has genial influences. It makes a bond of union between enemies. Governor Wise of Virginia, in the record of his first interviews with his prisoner, appeared to great advantage. If Governor Wise is a superior man, or inasmuch as he is a superior man, he distinguishes John Brown. As they confer, they understand each other swiftly; each respects the other. If opportunity allowed, they would prefer each other's society and desert their former companions. Enemies would become affectionate. Hector and Achilles, Richard and Saladin, Wellington and Soult, General Daumas and Abdel-Kader, become aware that they are nearer and more alike than any other two, and, if their nation and circumstance did not keep them apart, would run into each other's arms.

See too what good contagion belongs to it. Everywhere it finds its own with magnetic affinity. Courage of the soldier awakes the courage of woman. Florence Nightingale brings lint and the blessing of her shadow. Heroic women offer themselves as nurses of the brave veteran. The troop of Virginian infantry that had marched to guard the prison of John Brown ask leave to pay their respects to the prisoner. Poetry and eloquence catch the hint, and soar to a pitch unknown before. Everything feels the new breath except the old doting nigh-dead politicians, whose heart the trumpet of resurrection could not wake.

The charm of the best courages is that they are inventions, inspirations, flashes of genius. The hero could not have done the feat at another hour, in a lower mood. The best act of the marvelous genius of Greece was its first act; not in the statue or the Parthenon, but in the instinct which, at Thermopylae, held Asia at bay, kept Asia out of Europe,—Asia with its antiquities and organic slavery,—from corrupting the hope and new morning of the West. The statue, the architecture, were the later and inferior creation of the same genius. In view of this moment of history, we recognize a certain prophetic instinct, better than wisdom. Napoleon said well, "My hand is immediately connected with my head;" but the sacred courage is connected with the heart. The head is a half, a fraction, until it is enlarged and inspired by the moral sentiment. For it is not the means on which we draw, as health or wealth, practical skill or dexterous talent, or multitudes of followers, that count, but the aims only. The aim reacts back on the means. A great aim aggrandizes the means. The meal and water that are the commissariat of the forlorn hope that stake their lives to defend the pass are sacred as the Holy Grail, or as if one had eyes to see in chemistry the fuel that is rushing to feed the sun.

There is a persuasion in the soul of man that he is here for cause, that he was put down in this place by the Creator to do the work for which he inspires him, that thus he is an overmatch for all antagonists that could combine against him. The pious Mrs. Hutchinson says of some passages in the defense of Nottingham against the Cavaliers, "It was a great instruction that the best and highest courages are beams of the Almighty." And whenever the religious sentiment is adequately affirmed, it must be with dazzling courage. As long as it is cowardly insinuated, as with the wish to succor some partial and temporary interest, or to make it affirm some pragmatical tenet which our parish church receives today, it is not imparted, and cannot inspire or create. For it is always new, leads and surprises, and practice never comes up with it. There are ever appearing in the world men who, almost as soon as they are born, take a bee-line to the rack of the inquisitor, the axe of the tyrant, like Giordano Bruno, Vanini, Huss, Paul, Jesus and Socrates. Look at Fox's Lives of the Martyrs, Sewel's History of the Quakers, Southey's Book of the Church, at the folios of the Brothers Bollandi, who collected the lives of twenty-five thousand martyrs, confessors, ascetics and self-tormentors. There is much of fable, but a broad basis of fact. The tender skin does not shrink from bayonets, the timid woman is not scared by fagots; the rack is not frightful, nor the rope ignominious. The poor Puritan, Antony Parsons, at the stake, tied straw on his head when the fire approached him, and said, "This is God's hat." Sacred courage indicates that a man loves an idea better than all things in the world; that he is aiming neither at riches nor comfort, but will venture all to put in act the invisible thought in his mind. He is everywhere a liberator, but of a freedom that is ideal; not seeking to have land or money or conveniences, but to have no other limitation than that which his own constitution imposes. He is free to speak truth; he is not free to lie. He wishes to break every yoke all over the world which hinders his brother from acting after his thought.

There are degrees of courage, and each step upward makes us acquainted with a higher virtue. Let us say then frankly that the education of the will is the object of our existence. Poverty, the prison, the rack, the fire, the hatred and execrations of our fellow men, appear trials beyond the endurance of common humanity; but to the hero whose intellect is aggrandized by the soul, and so measures these penalties against the good which his thought surveys, these terrors vanish as darkness at sunrise.

We have little right in piping times of peace to pronounce on these rare heights of character; but there is no assurance of security. In the most private life, difficult duty is never far off. Therefore we must think with courage. Scholars and thinkers are prone to an effeminate habit, and shrink if a coarser shout comes up from the street, or a brutal act is recorded in the journals. The Medical College piles up in its museum its grim monsters of morbid anatomy, and there are melancholy skeptics with a taste for carrion who batten on the hideous facts in history,—persecutions, inquisitions, St. Bartholomew massacres, devilish lives, Nero, Caesar Borgia, Marat, Lopez; men in whom every ray of humanity was extinguished, parricides, matricides and whatever moral monsters. These are not cheerful facts, but they do not disturb a healthy mind; they require of us a patience as robust as the energy that attacks us, and an unresting exploration of final causes. Wolf, snake and crocodile are not inharmonious in Nature, but are made useful as checks, scavengers and pioneers; and we must have a scope as large as Nature's to deal with beast-like men, detect what scullion function is assigned them, and foresee in the secular melioration of the planet how these will become unnecessary and will die out.

He has not learned the lesson of life who does not every day surmount a fear. I do not wish to put myself or any man into a theatrical position, or urge him to ape the courage of his comrade. Have the courage not to adopt another's courage. There is scope and cause and resistance enough for us in our proper work and circumstance. And there is no creed of an honest man, be he Christian, Turk or Gentoo, which does not equally preach it. If you have no faith in beneficent power above you, but see only an adamantine fate coiling its folds about Nature and man, then reflect that the best use of fate is to teach us courage, if only because baseness cannot change the appointed event. If you accept your thoughts as inspirations from the Supreme Intelligence, obey them when they prescribe difficult duties, because they come only so long as they are used; or, if your skepticism reaches to the last verge, and you have no confidence in any foreign mind, then be brave, because there is one good opinion which must always be of consequence to you, namely, your own.

Emerson's Keys to Success

*Self-sacrifice is the real miracle
out of which all the reported miracles grew.*

The measure of our sincerity and therefore of the respect of men, is the amount of health and wealth we will hazard in the defense of our right.

They can conquer who believe they can.

Pain is superficial, and therefore fear is.

*True courage is not ostentatious; men who wish to inspire terror
seem thereby to confess themselves cowards.*

*Sacred courage indicates that a man loves an idea better than
all things in the world; that he is aiming neither at riches nor comfort,
but will venture all to put in act the invisible thought in his mind.*

*He has not learned the lesson of life
who does not every day surmount a fear.*

*I*nspiration

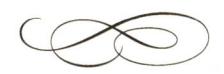

That flowing river, which, out of regions I see not,
Pours for a season its streams into me.

It was Watt who told King George III that he dealt in an article of which kings were said to be fond, Power. 'Tis certain that the one thing we wish to know is, where power is to be bought. But we want a finer kind than that of commerce; and every reasonable man would give a n y price of house and land and future pro vision, for condensation, concentration and the recalling at will of high mental energy. Our money is only a second best. We would jump to buy power with it, that is, intellectual perception moving the will. That is first best. But we don't know where the shop is. If Watt knew, he forgot to tell us the number of the street. There are times when the intellect is so active that everything seems to run to meet it. Its supplies are found without much thought as to studies. Knowledge runs to the man, and the man runs to knowledge. In spring, when the snow melts, the maple-trees flow with sugar, and you cannot get tubs fast enough; but it is only for a few days. The hunter on the prairie, at the right season, has no need of choosing his ground; east, west, by the river, by the timber, he is everywhere near his game. But the favorable conditions are rather the exception than the rule.

The aboriginal man, in geology and in the dim light of Darwin's microscope, is not an engaging figure. We are very glad that he ate his fishes and snails and marrow-bones out of our sight and hearing, and that his doleful experiences were got through with so very long ago. They combed his mane, they pared his nails, cut off his tail, set him on end, sent him to school and made him pay taxes, before he could begin to write his sad story for the compassion or the repudiation of his descendants, who are all but unanimous to disown him. We must take him as we find him,— pretty well on in his education, and, in all *our* knowledge of him, an interesting creature with a will, an invention, an imagination, a con science and an inextinguishable hope.

The Hunterian law of *arrested development* is not confined to vegetable and animal structure, but reaches the human intellect also. In the savage man, thought is infantile; and, in the civilized, unequal and ranging up and down a long scale. In the best races it is rare and imperfect. In happy moments it is reinforced, and carries out what were rude suggestions to larger scope and to clear and grand conclusions. The poet cannot see a natural phenomenon which does not express to him correspondent fact in his mental experience; he is made aware of a power to carry on and complete the metamorphosis of natural into spiritual facts. Everything which we hear for the first time was expected by the mind: the newest discovery was expected. In the mind we call this enlarged power Inspiration. I believe that nothing great and lasting can be done except by inspiration, by leaning on the secret augury. The man's insight and power are interrupted and occasional; he can see and do this or that cheap task, at will, but it steads him not beyond. He is fain to make the ulterior step by mechanical means. It cannot so be done, That ulterior step is to be also by inspiration; if not through him, then by another man. Every real step is by what a poet called "lyrical glances," by lyrical facility, and never by main strength and ignorance. Years of mechanic toil will only seem to do it; it will not so be done.

Inspiration is like yeast. 'Tis is no matter in which of half a dozen ways you procure the infection; you can apply one or the other equally well to your purpose, and get your loaf of bread. And every earnest workman, in whatever kind, knows some favorable conditions for his task. When I wish to write on any topic, 'tis of no consequence what kind of book or man gives me a hint or a motion, nor how far off that is from my topic.

Power is the first good. Rarey can tame a wild horse; but if he could give speed to a dull horse, were not that better? The toper finds, without asking, the road to the tavern, but the poet does not know the pitcher that holds his nectar. Every youth should know the way to prophecy as surely as the miller understands how to let on the water or the engineer the steam. A rush of thoughts is the only conceivable prosperity that can come to us. Fine clothes, equipages, villa, park, social consideration, cannot cover up real poverty and insignificance, from my own eyes or from others like mine

Thoughts let us into realities. Neither miracle nor magic nor any religious tradition, not the immortality of the private soul is incredible, after we have experienced an insight, a thought. I think it comes to some men but once in their life, sometimes a religious impulse, sometimes an intellectual insight. But what we want is consecutiveness. 'Tis with us a flash of light, then a long darkness, then a flash again. The separation of our days by sleep almost destroys identity. Could we but turn these fugitive sparkles into an astronomy of Copernican worlds! With most men, scarce a link of memory holds yesterday and today together. Their house and trade and families serve them as ropes to give a coarse continuity. But they have forgotten the thoughts of yesterday; they say to day what occurs to them, and something else tomorrow. This insecurity of posses sion, this quick ebb of power,— as if life were a thunder storm wherein you can see by a flash the horizon, and then cannot see your hand,—tantalizes us. We cannot make the inspiration consecutive. A glimpse, a point of view that by its brightness excludes the purview is granted, but no panorama. A fuller inspiration should cause the point to flow and become a line, should bend the line and complete the circle. Today the electric machine will not work, no spark will pass; then presently the world is all a cat's back, all sparkle and shock. Sometimes there is no sea-fire, and again the sea is aglow to the horizon. Sometimes the Aeolian harp is dumb all day in the window, and again it is garrulous and tells all the secrets of the world. In June the morning is noisy with birds; in August they are already getting old and silent.

Hence arises the question, Are these moods in any degree within control? If we knew how to command them! But where is the Franklin with kite or rod for this fluid?—a Franklin who can draw off electricity from

Jove himself, and convey it into the arts of life, in spire men, take them off their feet, withdraw them from the life of trifles and gain and comfort, and make the world transparent, so that they can read the symbols of Nature? What metaphysician has undertaken to enumerate the tonics of the torpid mind, the rules for the recovery of inspiration? That is least within control which is best in them. Of the *modus* of inspiration we have no knowledge. But in the experience of meditative men there is a certain agreement as to the conditions of reception. Plato, in his seventh Epistle, notes that the perception is only accomplished by long familiarity with the objects of intellect, and a life according to the things themselves. "Then a light, as if leaping from a fire, will on a sudden be enkindled in the soul, and will then itself nourish itself." He said again, "The man who is his own master knocks in vain at the doors of poetry." The artists must be sacrificed to their art. Like bees, they must put their lives into the sting they give. What is a man good for without enthusiasm? and what is enthusiasm but this daring of ruin for its object? There are thoughts beyond the reaches of our souls; we are not the less drawn to them. The moth flies into the flame of the lamp; and Swedenborg must solve the problems that haunt him, though he be crazed or killed.

There is genius as well in virtue as in intellect. 'Tis the doctrine of faith over works. The raptures of goodness are as old as history and new with this morning's sun. The legends of Arabia, Persia and India are of the same complexion as the Christian. Socrates, Menu, Confucius, Zertusht,— we recognize in all of them this ardor to solve the hints of thought.

I hold that ecstasy will be found normal, or only an example on a higher plane of the same gentle gravitation by which stones fall and rivers run. Experience identifies. Shakespeare seems to you miraculous; but the wonderful juxtapositions, parallelisms, transfers, which his genius effected, were all to him locked together as links of a chain, and the mode precisely as conceivable and familiar to higher intelligence as the index-making of the literary hack. The result of the hack is inconceivable to the type-setter who waits for it.

We must prize our own youth. Later, we want heat to execute our plans: the good will, the knowledge, the whole armory of means are all present, but a certain heat that once used not to fail, refuses its office, and all is vain until this capricious fuel is supplied. It seems a semi-animal heat; as if tea, or wine, or sea-air, or mountains, or a genial companion, or a new thought suggested in book or conversation could fire the train, wake the fancy and the clear perception. Pit-coal,—where to find it? 'Tis of no use that your engine is made like a watch,—that you are a good workman, and know how to drive it, if there is no coal. We are waiting until some tyrannous idea emerging out of heaven shall seize and bereave us of this liberty with which we are falling abroad. Well, we have the same hint or suggestion, day by day. "I am not," says the man, "at the top of my condition today, but the favorable hour will come when I can command all my powers, and when that will be easy to do which is at this moment impossible." See how the passions augment our force,—anger, love, ambition'—sometimes sympathy, and the expectation of men. Garrick said that on the stage his great paroxysms surprised himself as much as his audience. If this is true on this low plane, it is true on the higher. Swedenborg's genius was the perception of the doctrine that "The Lord flows into the spirits of angels and of men;" and all poets have signalized their consciousness of rare moments when they were superior to themselves,—when a light, a freedom, a power came to them which lifted them to performances far better than they could reach at other times; so that a religious poet once told me that he valued his poems, not because they were his, but because they were not. He thought the angels brought them to him.

Jacob Behmen said: "Art has not wrote here, nor was there any time to consider how to set it punctually down according to the right understanding of the letters, but all was ordered according to the direction of the spirit, which often went on haste,—so that the penman's hand, by reason he was not accustomed to it, did often shake. And, though I could have written in a more accurate, fair and plain manner, the burning fire often forced forward with speed, and the hand and pen must hasten directly after it, for it comes and goes as a sudden shower. In one quarter of an hour I saw and knew more than if I had been many years together at an university."

The depth of the notes which we accidentally sound on the strings of Nature is out of all proportion to our taught and ascertained faculty, and might teach us what strangers and novices we are, vagabond in this universe of pure power, to which we have only the smallest key. Herrick said:—

> " 'Tis not every day that I
> Fitted am to prophesy;
> No, but when the spirit fills
> The fantastic panicles,
> Full of fire, then I write
> As the Godhead doth indite.
> Thus enraged, my lines are hurled,
> Like the Sibyl's, through the world:
> Look how next the holy fire
> Either slakes, or doth retire;
> So the fancy cools.—till when
> That brave spirit comes again."

Bonaparte said: "There is no man more Pusillanimous than I, when I make a military plan. I magnify all the dangers, and all the possible mischances. I am in an agitation utterly painful. That does not prevent me from appearing quite serene to the persons who surround me. I am like a woman with child, and when my resolution is taken, all is forgot except whatever can make it succeed."

There are, to be sure, certain risks in this presentment of the decisive perception, as in the use of ether or alcohol:

> "Great wits to madness nearly are allied;
> Both serve to make our poverty our pride."

Aristotle said: "No great genius was ever without some mixture of madness, nor can anything grand or superior to the voice of common mortals be spoken except by the agitated soul." We might say of these memorable moments of life that we were in them, not they in us. We found our selves by happy for tune in an illuminated portion of meteorous zone, and passed o u t of it again, so aloof was it from any will of ours. "It is a principle of war," said Napoleon, "that when you can use the lightning it is better than cannon."

How many sources of inspiration can we count? As many as our affinities. But to a practical purpose we may reckon a few of these.

I. Health is the first muse, comprising the magical benefits of air, landscape and bodily exercise, on the mind. The Arabs say that "Allah does not count from life the days spent in the chase," that is, those are thrown in. Plato thought "exercise would almost cure a guilty conscience." Sydney Smith said: "You will never break down in a speech on the day when you have walked twelve miles."

I honor health as the first muse, and sleep as the condition of health. Sleep benefits mainly by the sound health it produces; incidentally also by dreams, into whose farrago a divine lesson is sometimes slipped. Life is in short cycles or periods; we are quickly tired, but we have rapid rallies. A man is spent by his work, starved, prostrate; he will not lift his hand to save his life; he can never think more. He sinks into deep sleep and wakes with renewed youth, with hope, courage, fertile in resources, and keen for daring adventure.

> "Sleep is like death, and after sleep
> The world seems new begun:
> White thoughts stand luminous and firm,
> Like statues in the sun;
> Refreshed from supersensuous founts,
> The soul to clearer vision mounts."

A man must be able to escape from his cares and fears, as well as from hunger and want of sleep; so that another Arabian proverb has its coarse truth: "When the belly is full, it says to the head, Sing, fellow!" The perfection of writing is when mind and body are both in key; when the mind finds perfect obedience in the body. And wine, no doubt, and all fine food, as of delicate fruits, furnish some elemental wisdom. And the fire, too, as it burns in the chimney; for I fancy that my logs, which have grown so long in sun and wind by Walden, are a kind of muses. So of all the particulars of health and exercise and fit nutriment and tonics. Some people will tell you there is a great deal of poetry and fine sentiment in a chest of tea.

2. The experience of writing letters is one of the keys to the *modus* of inspiration. When we have ceased for a long time to have any fulness of thoughts that once made a diary a joy as well as a necessity, and have come to believe that an image or a happy turn of expression is no longer at our command, in writing a letter to a friend we may find that we rise to thought and to a cordial power of expression that costs no effort, and it seems to us that this facility may be indefinitely applied and resumed. The wealth of the mind in this respect of seeing is like that of a looking-glass, which is never tired or worn by any multitude of objects which it reflects, You may carry it all round the world, it is ready and perfect as ever for new millions.

3. Another consideration, though it will not so much interest young men, will cheer the heart of older scholars, namely that there is diurnal and secular rest. As there is this daily renovation of sensibility, so it sometimes if rarely happens that after a season of decay or eclipse, darkening months or years, the faculties revive to their fullest force. One of the best facts I know in metaphysical science is Niebuhr's joyful record that after his genius for interpreting history had failed him for several years, this divination returned to him, As this rejoiced me, so does Herbert's poem "The Flower." His health had broken down early, he had lost his muse, and in this poem he says:

> "And now in age I bud again,
> After so many deaths I live and write:
> I once more smell the dew and rain,
> And relish versing: O my only light,
> It cannot be
> That I am he
> On whom thy tempests fell all night."

His poem called "The Forerunners" also has supreme interest. I understand The Harbingers to refer to the signs of age and decay which he detects in himself, not only in his constitution, but in his fancy and his facility and grace in writing verse; and he signalizes his delight in this skill, and his pain that the Herricks, Lovelaces and Marlowes, or whoever else, should use the like genius in language to sensual purpose, and consoles himself that his own faith and the divine life in him remain to him unchanged, unharmed.

4. The power of the will is sometimes sublime; and what is will for, if it cannot help us in emergencies? Seneca says of an almost fatal sickness that befell him, "The thought of my father, who could not have sustained such a blow as my death, restrained me; I commanded myself to live." Goethe said to Eckermann, "I work more easily when the barometer is high than when it is low. Since I know this, I endeavor, when the barometer is low, to counteract the injurious effect by greater exertion, and my attempt is successful."

"To the persevering mortal the blessed immortals are swift." Yes, for they know how to give you in one moment the solution of the riddle you have pondered for months. "Had I not lived with Mirabeau," says Dumont, "I never should have known all that can be done in one day, or, rather, in an interval of twelve hours. A day to him was of more value than a week or a month to others. Tomorrow to him was not the same impostor as to most others."

5. Plutarch affirms that "souls are naturally endowed with the faculty of prediction, and the chief cause that excites this faculty and virtue is a certain temperature of air and winds." My anchorite thought it "sad that atmospheric influences should bring to our dust the communion of the soul with the Infinite." But I am glad that the atmosphere should be an excitant, glad to find the dull rock itself to be deluged with Deity, to be theist, Christian, poetic. The fine influences of the morning few can explain, but all will admit.

The French have a proverb to the effect that not the day only, but all things have their morning, —"*Il n'y a que le matin en routes choses.*" And it is a primal rule to defend your morning, to keep all its dews on, and with fine foresight to relieve it from any jangle of affairs—even from the question, Which task? I remember a capital prudence of old President Quincy, who told me that he never went to bed at night until he had laid out the studies for the next morning. I believe that in our good days a well-ordered mind has a new thought awaiting it every morning. And hence, eminently thoughtful men, from the time of Pythagoras down, have insisted on an hour of solitude every day, to meet their own mind and learn what oracle it has to impart. If a new view of life or mind gives us joy, so does new arrangement. I don't know but we take as much delight, in finding the right place for an old observation, as in a new thought.

6. Solitary converse with Nature; for thence are ejaculated sweet and dreadful words never uttered in libraries. Ah! the spring days, the summer dawns, the October woods! I confide that my reader knows these delicious secrets, has perhaps

> Slighted Minerva's learned tongue,
> But leaped with joy when on the wind the shell
> of Clio rung.

Are you poetical, impatient of trade, tired of labor and affairs? Do you want Monadnoc, Agiocochook, or Helvellyn, or Plinlimmon, dear to English song, in your closet? Caerleon, Provence, Ossian and Cadwallon? Tie a couple of strings across a board and set it in your window, and you have an instrument which no artist's harp can rival. It needs no instructed ear; if you have sensibility, it admits you to sacred interiors; it has the sadness of Nature, yet, at the changes, tones of triumph and festal notes ringing out all measures of loftiness. "Did you never observe," says Gray, "'while rocking winds are piping loud,' that pause, as the gust is recollecting itself, and rising upon the ear in a shrill and plaintive note, like the swell of an Aeolian harp? I do assure you there is nothing in the world so like the voice of a spirit." Perhaps you can recall a delight like it, which spoke to the eye, when you have stood by a lake in the woods in summer, and saw where little flaws of wind whip spots or patches of still water into fleets of ripples,—so sudden, so slight, so spiritual, that it was more like the rippling of the Aurora Borealis at night than any spectacle of day.

7. But the solitude of Nature is not so essential as solitude of habit. I have found my advantage in going in summer to a country inn, in winter to a city hotel, with a task which would not prosper at home. I thus secured a more absolute seclusion; for it is almost impossible for a housekeeper who is in the country a small farmer, to exclude interruptions and even necessary orders, though I bar out by system all I can, and resolutely omit, to my constant damage, all that can be omitted. At home, the day is cut into short strips. In the hotel, I have no hours to keep, no visits to make or receive, and I command an astronomic leisure. I forget rain, wind, cold and heat. At home, I remember in my library the wants of the farm, and have all too much sympathy. I envy the abstraction of some scholars I have known, who could sit on a curbstone in State Street, put up their back, and solve their problem. I have more womanly eyes. All the conditions must be right for my success, slight as that is. What untunes is as bad as what cripples or stuns me. Novelty, surprise, change of scene, refresh the artist,—"break up the tiresome old roof of heaven into new forms," as Hafiz said. The seashore and the taste of two metals in contact, and our enlarged powers in the presence, or rather at the approach and at the departure of a friend, and the mixture of lie in truth, and the experience of poetic creativeness which is not found in staying at home nor yet in traveling, but in transitions from one to the other, which must therefore be adroitly managed to present as much transitional surface as possible,—these are the types or conditions of this power. "A ride near the sea, a sail near the shore," said the ancient. So Montaigne travelled with his books, but did not read in them. *"La Nature aime les croisements,"* says Fourier.

I know there is room for whims here; but in regard to some apparent trifles there is great agreement as to their annoyance. And the machine with which we are dealing is of such an inconceivable delicacy that whims also must be respected. Fire must lend its aid. We not only want time, but warm time. George Sand says, "I have no enthusiasm for Nature which the slightest chill will not I instantly destroy." And I remember Thoreau, with his robust will, yet found certain trifles disturbing the delicacy of that health which composition exacted,—namely, the slightest irregularity, even to the drinking too much water on the preceding day. Even a steel pen is a nuisance to some writers. Some of us may remember, years ago, in the English journals, the petition, signed by Carlyle, Browning, Tennyson, Dickens and other writers in London, against the license of the organ-grinders, who infested the streets near their houses, to levy on them blackmail.

Certain localities, as mountain-tops, the seaside, the shores of rivers and rapid brooks, natural parks of oak and pine, where the ground is smooth and unencumbered, are excitants of the muse. Every artist knows well some favorite retirement. And yet the experience of some good artists has taught them to prefer the smallest and plainest chamber, with one chair and table and with no outlook, to these picturesque liberties. William Blake said, "Natural objects always did and do weaken, deaden and obliterate imagination in me." And Sir Joshua Reynolds had no pleasure in Richmond; he used to say "the human face was his landscape." These indulgences are to be used with great caution. Allston rarely left his studio by day. An old friend took him, one fine afternoon, a spacious circuit into the country, and he painted two or three pictures as the fruits of that drive, But he made it a rule not to go to the city on two consecutive days. One was rest; more was lost time. The times of force must be well husbanded, and the wise student will remember the prudence of Sir Tristram in *Morte d'Arthur,* who, having received from the fairy an enchantment of six hours of growing strength every day, took care to fight in the hours when his strength increased; since from noon to night his strength abated. What prudence again does every artist, every scholar need in the security of his easel or his desk! These must be remote from the work of the house, and from all knowledge of the feet that come and go therein. Allston, it is said, had two or three rooms in different parts of Boston, where he could not be found. For the delicate muses lose their head if their attention is once diverted. Perhaps if you were successful abroad in talking and dealing with men, you would not come back to your book-shelf and your task. When the spirit chooses you for its scribe to publish some commandment, it makes you odious to men and men odious to you, and you shall accept that loathsomeness with joy. The moth must fly to the lamp, and you must solve those questions though you die.

8. Conversation, which, when it is best, is a series of intoxications. Not Aristotle, not Kant or Hegel, but conversation, is the right metaphysical professor. This is the true school of philosophy,—this the college where you learn what thoughts are, what powers lurk in those fugitive gleams, and what becomes of them; how they make history. A wise man goes to this game to play upon others and to be played upon, and at least as curious to know what can be drawn from himself as what can be drawn from them. For, in discourse with a friend, our thought, hitherto wrapped in our consciousness, detaches itself, and allows itself to be seen as a thought, in a manner as new and entertaining to us as to our companions. For provocation of thought, we use ourselves and use each other. Some perceptions—I think the best—are granted to the single soul; they come from the depth and go to the depth and are the permanent and controlling ones. Others it takes two to find. We must be warmed by the fire of sympathy, to be brought into the right conditions and angles of vision. Conversation; for intellectual activity is contagious. We are emulous. If the tone of the companion is higher than ours, we delight in rising to it. 'Tis a historic observation that a writer must find an audience up to his thought, or he will no longer care to impart it, but will sink to their level or be silent. Homer said, "When two come together, one apprehends before the other;" but it is because one thought well that the other thinks better: and two men of good mind will excite each other's activity, each attempting still to cap the other's thought. In enlarged conversation we have suggestions that require new ways of living, new books, new men, new arts and sciences. By sympathy, each opens to the eloquence, and begins to see with the eyes of his mind. We were all lonely, thoughtless; and now a principle appears to all: we see new relations, many truths; every mind seizes them as they pass; each catches by the mane one of these strong coursers like horses of the prairie, and rides up and down in the world of the intellect. We live

day by day under the illusion that it is the fact or event that imports, whilst really it is not that which signifies, but the use we put it to, or what we think of it. We esteem nations important, until we discover that a few individuals much more concern us; then, later, that it is not at last a few individuals, or any sacred heroes, but the lowliness, the outpouring, the large equality to truth of a single mind,—as if in the narrow walls of a human heart the whole realm of truth, the world of morals, the tribunal by which the universe is judged, found room to exist.

9. New poetry; by which I mean chiefly, old poetry that is new to the reader. I have heard from persons who had practice in rhyming, that it was sufficient to set them on writing verses, to read any original poetry. What is best in literature is the affirming, prophesying, spermatic words of men-making poets. Only that is poetry which cleanses and mans me.

Words used in a new sense and figuratively, dart a delightful luster; and *every* word admits a new use, and hints ulterior meanings. We have not learned the law of the mind,—cannot control and domesticate at will the high states of contemplation and continuous thought. "Neither by sea nor by land," said Pindar, "canst thou find the way to the Hyperboreans;" neither by idle wishing, nor by rule of three or rule of thumb. Yet I find a mitigation or solace by providing always a good book for my journeys, as Horace or Martial or Goethe,—some book which lifts me quite out of prosaic surroundings, and from which I draw some lasting knowledge. A Greek epigram out of the anthology, a verse of Herrick or Lovelace, are in harmony both with sense and spirit.

You shall not read newspapers, nor politics, nor novels, nor Montaigne, nor the newest French book. You may read Plutarch, Plato, Plotinus, Hindoo mythology and ethics. You may read Chaucer, Shakespeare, Ben Jonson, Milton, and Milton's prose as his verse; read Collins and Gray; read Hafiz and the Trouveurs; nay, Welsh and British mythology of Arthur, and (in your ear) Ossian; fact-books, which all geniuses prize as raw material, and as antidote to verbiage and false poetry. Fact-books, if the facts be well and thoroughly told, are much more nearly allied to poetry than many books are that are written in rhyme. Only our newest knowledge works as a source of inspiration and thought, as only the outmost layer of *liber* on the tree. Books of natural science, especially those written by the ancients,—geography, botany, agriculture, explorations of the sea, of meteors, of astronomy,—all the better if written without literary aim or ambition. Every book is good to read which sets the reader in a working mood. The deep book, no matter how remote the subject, helps us best.

Neither are these all the sources, nor can I name all. The receptivity is rare. The occasions or predisposing circumstances I could never tabulate; but now one, now another landscape, form, color, or companion, or perhaps one kind of sounding word or syllable, "strikes the electric chain with which we are darkly bound," and it is impossible to detect and willfully repeat the fine conditions to which we have owed our happiest frames of mind. The day is good in which we have had the most perceptions. The analysis is the more difficult, because poppy-leaves are strewn when a generalization is made; for I can never remember the circumstances to which I owe it, so as to repeat the experiment or put myself in the conditions:—

> " 'Tis the most difficult of tasks to keep
> Heights which the soul is competent to gain."

I value literary biography for the hints it furnishes from so many scholars, in so many countries, of what hygiene, what ascetic, what gymnastic, what social practices their experience suggested and approved. They are, for the most part, men who needed only a little wealth. Large estates, political relations, great hospitalities, would have been impediments to them. They are men whom a book could entertain, a new thought intoxicate and hold them prisoners for years perhaps. Aubrey and Burton and Wood tell me incidents which I find not insignificant.

These are some hints towards what is in all education a chief necessity,—the right government, or, shall I not say? the right obedience to the powers of the human soul. Itself is the dictator: the mind itself the awful oracle. All our power, all our happiness consists in our reception of its hints, which ever become clearer and grander as they are obeyed.

Emerson's Keys to Success

Nothing great and lasting can be done except by inspiration.

What is a man good for without enthusiasm?

Health is the first muse, comprising the magical benefits of air, landscape and bodily exercise, on the mind.

Writing letters is one of the keys to the **modus** *of inspiration.*

"To the persevering mortal the blessed immortals are swift."

I believe that in our good days a well-ordered mind has a new thought awaiting it every morning.

Eminently thoughtful men, from the time of Pythagoras down, have insisted on an hour of solitude every day, to meet their own mind and learn what oracle it has to impart.

Conversation is the true school of philosophy.

Intellectual activity is contagious.

Resources

Go where he will, the wise man is at home,
His hearth is the earth,—his hall the azure dome;
Where his clear spirit leads him, there's his road,
By God's own light illumined and foreshowed.

MEN ARE MADE UP of potencies. We are magnets in an iron globe. We have keys to all doors. We are all inventors, each sailing out on a voyage of discovery, guided each by a private chart, of which there is no duplicate. The world is all gates, all opportunities, strings of tension waiting to be struck; the earth sensitive as iodine to light; the most plastic and impressionable medium, alive to every touch, and, whether searched by the plough of Adam, the sword of Caesar, the boat of Columbus, the telescope of Galileo, or the surveyor's chain of Picard, or the submarine telegraph, to every one of these experiments it makes a gracious response. I am benefited by every observation of a victory of man over nature,—by seeing that wisdom is better than strength; by seeing that every healthy and resolute man is an organizer, a method coming into a confusion and drawing order out of it. We are touched and cheered by every such example. We like to see the inexhaustible riches of Nature, and the access of every soul to her magazines. These examples wake an infinite hope, and call every man to emulation. A low, hopeless spirit puts out the eyes; skepticism is slow suicide. A philosophy which sees only the worst; believes neither in virtue nor in genius; which says 'tis all of no use, life is eating us up, 'tis only question who shall be last devoured,—dispirits us; the sky shuts down before us. A Schopenhauer, with logic and learning and wit, teaching pessimism,—teaching that this is the worst of all possible worlds, and inferring that sleep is better than waking, and death than sleep,—all the talent in the world cannot save him from being odious. But if, instead of these negatives, you give me affirmatives,—if you tell me that there is always life for the living; that what man has done man can do; that this world belongs to the energetic; that there is always a way to everything desirable; that every man is provided, in the new bias of his faculty, with a key to nature, and that man only rightly knows himself as far as he has experimented on things,—I am invigorated, put into genial and working temper; the horizon opens, and we are full of good-will and gratitude to the Cause of Causes. I like the sentiment of the poor woman who, coming from a wretched garret in an inland manufacturing town for the first time to the sea-shore, gazing at the ocean, said "she was glad for once in her life to see something which there was enough of."

Our Copernican globe is a great factory or shop of power, with its rotating constellations, times, and tides. The machine is of colossal size; the diameter of the water-wheel, the arms of the levers, and the volley of the battery, out of all mechanic measure; and it takes long to understand its parts and its workings. This pump never sucks; these screws are never loose; this machine is never out of gear. The vat, the piston, the wheels and tires, never wear out, but are self-repairing. Is there any load which water cannot lift? If there be, try steam; or if not that, try electricity. Is there any exhausting of these means? Measure by barrels the spending of the brook that runs through your field. Nothing is great but the inexhaustible wealth of Nature. She shows us only surfaces, but she is million fathoms deep. What spaces! what durations! dealing with races as merely preparations of somewhat to follow; or, in humanity, millions of lives of men to collect the first observations on which our astronomy is built; millions of lives to add only sentiments and guesses, which at last, gathered in by an ear of sensibility, make the furniture of the poet. See how children build up a language; how every traveller, every laborer, every impatient boss, who sharply shortens the phrase or the word to give his order quicker, reducing it to the lowest possible terms,—and there it must stay,—improves the national tongue. What power does Nature not owe to her duration of amassing infinitesimals into cosmical forces!

The marked events in history, as the emigration of a colony to a new and more delightful coast; the building of a large ship; the discovery of the mariner's compass, which perhaps the Phoenicians made; the arrival among an old stationary nation of a more instructed race, with new arts: each of these events electrifies the tribe to which it befalls; supplies the tough barbarous sinew, and brings it into that state of sensibility which makes the transition to civilization possible and sure. By his machines man can dive and remain under water like a shark; can fly like a hawk in the air; can see atoms like a gnat; can see the system of the universe like Uriel, the angel of the sun; can carry whatever loads a ton of coal can lift; can knock down cities with his fist of gunpowder; can recover the history of his race by the medals which the deluge, and every creature, civil or savage or brute, has involuntarily dropped of its existence; and divine the future possibility of the planet and its inhabitants by his perception of laws of nature. Ah! what a plastic little creature he is! so shifty, so adaptive! his body a chest of tools, and he making himself comfortable in every climate, in every condition.

Here in America are all the wealth of soil, of timber, of mines, and of the sea, put into the pos? session of a people who wield all these wonderful machines, have the secret of steam, of electricity, and have the power and habit of invention in their brain. We Americans have got suppled into the state of melioration. Life is always rapid here, but what acceleration to its pulse in ten years,—what in the four years of the war! We have seen the railroad and telegraph subdue our enormous geography; we have seen the snowy deserts on the northwest, seats of Eskimo, be-come lands of promise. When our population, swarming west, had reached the boundary of arable land, as if to stimulate our energy, on the face of the sterile waste beyond, the land was suddenly in parts found covered with gold and silver, floored with coal. It was thought a fable, what Guthrie, a traveller in Persia, told us, that " in Taurida, in any piece of ground where springs of naphtha (or petroleum) obtain, by merely sticking an iron tube in the earth, and applying a light to the upper end, the mineral oil will burn till the tube is decomposed, or for a vast number of years." But we have found the Taurida in Pennsylvania and Ohio. If they have not the lamp of Aladdin, they have the Aladdin oil. Resources of America! why, one thinks of St. Simon's saying, "The Golden Age is not behind, but before you." Here is man in the Garden ,of Eden; here the Genesis and the Exodus. We have seen slavery disappear like a painted scene in a theatre; we have seen the most healthful revolution in the politics of the nation, -the Constitution not only amended, but construed in a new spirit. We have seen China opened to European and American ambassadors and commerce; the like in Japan: our arts and productions begin to penetrate both. As the walls of a modern house are perforated with water-pipes, sound-pipes, gas-pipes, heat-pipes, so geography and geology are yielding to man's convenience, and we begin to perforate and mould the old ball, as a carpenter does with wood. All is ductile and plastic. We are working the new Atlantic telegraph. American energy is overriding every venerable maxim of political science. America is such a garden of plenty, such a magazine of power, that at her shores all the common rules of political economy utterly fail. Here is bread, and wealth, and power, and education for every man who has the heart to use his opportunity. The creation of power had never any parallel. It was thought that the immense production of gold would make gold cheap as pewter. But the immense expansion of trade has wanted every ounce of gold, and it has not lost its value.

See how nations of customers are formed. The disgust of California has not been able to drive nor kick the Chinaman back to his home; and now it turns out that he has sent home to China American food and tools and luxuries, until he has taught his people to use them, and a new market has grown up for our commerce. The emancipation has brought a whole nation of negroes as customers to buy all the articles which once their few masters bought, and every manufacturer and producer in the North has an interest in protecting the negro as the consumer of his wares.

The whole history of our civil war is rich in a thousand anecdotes attesting the fertility of resource, the presence of mind, the skilled labor of our people. At Annapolis a regiment, hastening to join the army, found the locomotives broken, the railroad destroyed, and no rails. The commander called for men in the ranks who could rebuild the road. Many men stepped forward, searched in the water, found the hidden rails, laid the tuck, put the disabled engine together, and continued their journey. The world belongs to the energetic man. His will gives him new eyes. He sees expedients and means where we saw none. The invalid sits shivering in lamb's-wool and furs; the woodsman knows how to make warm garments out of cold and wet themselves. The Indian, the sailor, the hunter, only these know the power of the hands, feet, teeth, eyes, and ears. It is out of the obstacles to be encountered that they make the means of destroying them. The sailor by his boat and sail makes a ford out of deepest waters. The hunter, the soldier, rolls himself in his blanket, and the falling snow, which he did not have to bring in his of Illinois, he overheard them say that they would scalp him. He said to them, "Will you scalp me? Here is my scalp," and confounded them by lifting a little periwig he wore. He then explained to them that he was a great medicine-man, and that they did great wrong in wishing to harm him, who carried them all in his heart. So he opened his shirt a little and showed to each of the savages in turn the reflection of his own eyeball in a small pocket-mirror which he had hung next to his skin. He assured them that if they should provoke him he would burn up their rivers and their forests; and, taking from his portmanteau a small phial of white brandy, he poured it into a cup, and, lighting a straw at the fire in the wigwam, he kindled the brandy (which they believed to be water), and burned it up before their eyes. Then taking up a chip of dry pine, he drew a burning glass from his pocket and set the chip on fire.

What a new face courage puts on everything! A determined man, by his very attitude and the tone of his voice, puts a stop to defeat, and begins to conquer. " For they can conquer who believe they can." Every one hears gladly that cheerful voice. He reveals to us the enormous power of one man over masses of men; that one man whose eye commands the end in view, and the means by which it can be attained, is not only better than ten men or a hundred men, but victor over all mankind who do not see the issue and the means. "When a man is once possessed with fear," said the old French Marshal Montloc, " and loses his judgment, as all men in a fright do, he knows not what he does. And it is the principal thing you are to beg at the hands of Almighty God, to preserve your understanding entire; for what danger soever there may be, there is still one way or other to get off, and perhaps to your honor. But when fear has once possessed you, God ye good even! You think you are flying toward the poop when you are running toward the prow, and for one enemy think you have ten before your eyes, as drunkards who see a thousand candles at once."

Against the terrors of the mob, which, intoxicated with passion, and once suffered to gain the ascendant, is diabolic and chaos come again, good sense has many arts of prevention and of relief. Disorganization is confronts with organization, with police, with military force. But in earlier stages of the disorder it applies milder and nobler remedies. The natural offset of terror is ridicule. And we have noted examples among our orators, who have on conspicuous occasions handled and controlled, and , best of all, converted a malignant mob, by superior manhood, and by a wit which disconcerted and at last delighted the ring-leaders. What can a poor truckman, who is hired to groan and hiss, do, when the orator shakes him into convulsions of laughter so that he cannot throw his egg? If a good story will not answer, still milder remedies sometimes serve to disperse a mob. Try sending round the contribution-box. Mr. Marshall, the eminent manufacturer at Leeds, was to preside at a Free Trade festival in that city; it was threatened that the operatives, who were in bad humor, would break up the meeting by a mob. Mr. MArshall was a man of peace; he had the pipes laid from the waterworks of his mill, with the stop-cock by his chair from which he could discharge a stream that would knock down an ox, and sat down very peacefully to his dinner, which was not disturbed.

See the dexterity of the good aunt in keeping the young people all the weary holiday busy and diverted without knowing it: the story, the pictures, the ballad, the game, the cuckoo-clock, the stereoscope, the rabbits, the mino bird, the pop-corn and Christmas hemlock spurting in the fire. The children never suspect how much design goes to it, and this unfailing fertility has been rehearsed a hundred times, when the necessity came of finding for the little Asmodeus a rope of sand to twist. She relies on the same principle that makes the strength of Newton,—alternation of employment. See how he refreshed himself, resting from the profound researches of the calculus by astronomy; from astronomy by optics; from optics by chronology. It is a law of chemistry that every gas is a vacuum to every other gas; and when the the mind has exhausted its energies for one employment, it is still fresh and capable of a different task. We have not a toy or trinket for idle amusement, but somewhere it is the one thing needful for solid instruction or to save the ship or army. In the Mammoth Cave in Kentucky, the torches which each traveller carries make a dismal funeral procession, and serve no purpose but to see the ground. When now and then the vaulted roof rises high overhead, and hides all its possibilities in lofty depths, 'tis is but gloom on gloom. But the guide kindled a Roman candle, and held it here and there shooting its fireballs successively into each crypt of the groined roof, disclosing its starry splendor, and showing for the first time what that plaything was good for.

Whether larger or less, these strokes and all exploits rest at last on the wonderful structure of the mind. And we learn that our doctrine of resources must be carried into higher application, namely, to the intellectual sphere. But every power in energy speedily arrives at its limits, and requires to be husbanded; the law of light, which Newton said proceeded by " fits of easy reflection and transmission"; the come-and-go of the pendulum is the law of mind; alternation of labors is its rest.

I should like to have the statistics of bold experimenting on the husbandry of mental power. In England men of letters drink wine; in Scotland, whiskey; in France, light wines; in Germany, beer. In England everybody rides in the saddle; in France the theatre and the ball occupy the night. In this country we have not learned how to repair the exhaustions of our climate. Is not the seaside necessary in summer? Games, fishing, bowling, hunting, gymnastics, dancing,—are not these needful to you? The chapter of pastimes is very long. There are better games than billiards and whist. 'Twas a pleasing trait in Goethe's romance, that Makaria retires from society " to astronomy and her correspondence."

I do not know that the treatise of Brillat Savarin on the Physiology of Taste deserves its fame. I know its repute, and I have heard it called the France of France. But the subject is so large and exigent that a few particulars, and those the pleasures of the epicure, cannot satisfy. I know many men of taste whose single opinions and practice would interest much more. It should be extended to gardens and grounds, and mainly one thing should be illustrated: that life in the country wants all things on a low tone,— wants coarse clothes, old shoes, no fleet horse that a man can-not hold, but an old horse that will stand tied in a pasture half a day without risk, so allowing the picnic-party the full freedom of the woods. Natural history is, in the country, most attractive; at once elegant, immortal, always opening new resorts. The first care of a man settling in the country should be to open the face of the earth to himself, by a little knowledge of nature, or a great deal, if he can, of birds, plants, rocks, astronomy; in short, the art of taking a walk. This will draw the sting out of frost, dreariness out of November and March, and the drowsiness out of August. To know the trees is, as Spenser says of "the ash, for nothing ill." Shells, too; how hungry I found myself, the other day, at Agassiz's Museum, for their names! But the uses of the woods are many, and some of them for the scholar high and peremptory. When his task requires the wiping out from memory

"all trivial fond records
That youth and observation copied there,"

he must leave the house, the streets, and the club, and go to wooded up-lands, to the clearing and the brook. Well for him if he can say with the old minstrel, " I know where to find a new song."

If I go into the woods in winter, and am shown the thirteen or fourteen species of willow that grow in Massachusetts, I learn that they quietly expand in the warmer days, or when nobody is looking at them, and, though insignificant enough in the general bareness of the forest, yet a great change takes place in them between fall and spring; in the first relentings of March they hasten, and long before anything else is ready, these osiers hangout their joyful flowers in contrast to all the woods. You cannot tell when they do bud and blossom, these vivacious trees, so ancient, for they are almost the oldest of all. Among fossil remains, the willow and the pine appear with the ferns. They bend all day to every wind; the cart-wheel in the road may crush them; every passenger may strike off a twig with his cane; every boy cuts them for a whistle; the cow, the rabbit, the insect, bite the sweet and tender bark; yet, in spite of accident and enemy, their gentle persistency lives when the oak is shattered by storm, and grows in the night and snow and cold. When I see in these brave plants this vigor and immortality in weakness, I find a sudden relief and pleasure in observing the mighty law of vegetation, and I think it more grateful and health-giving than any news I am likely to find of man in the journals, and better than Washington politics.

It is easy to see that there is no limit to the chapter of Resources. I have not, in all these rambling sketches, gone beyond the beginning of my list. Resources of Man,—it is the inventory of the world, the roll of arts and sciences; it is the whole of memory, the whole of invention; it is all the power of passion, the majesty of virtue, and the omnipotence of will.

But the one fact that shines through all this plenitude of powers is, that, as is the receiver, so is the gift; that all these acquisitions are victories of the good brain and brave heart; that the world belongs to the energetic, belongs to the wise. It is in vain to make a paradise but for good men. The tropics are one vast garden; yet man is more miserably fed and conditioned there than in the cold and stingy zones. The healthy, the civil, the industrious, the learned, the moral race,—Nature herself only yields her secret to these. And the resources of America and its future will be immense only to wise and virtuous men.

Emerson's Keys to Success

The world belongs to the energetic.

Here [in America] is bread, and wealth, and power, and education for every man who has the heart to use his opportunity.

A determined man, by his very attitude and the tone of his voice, puts a stop to defeat, and begins to conquer.

Leave the house, the streets, and the club, and go to wooded uplands, to the clearing and the brook.

Resources of Man,—it is the inventory of the world, the roll of arts and sciences; it is the whole of memory, the whole of invention; it is all the power of passion, the majesty of virtue, and the omnipotence of will.

Success

Our American people cannot be taxed with slowness in performance or in praising their performance. The earth is shaken by our energies. We are feeling our youth and nerve and bone. We have the power of territory and of seacoast, and know the use of these. We count our census, we read our growing valuations, we survey our map, which becomes old in a year or two. Our eyes run approvingly along the lengthened lines of railroad and telegraph. We have gone nearest to the Pole. We have discovered the Antarctic continent. We interfere in Central and South America, at Canton and in Japan; we are adding to an already enormous territory. Our political constitution is the hope of the world, and we value ourselves on all these feats.

'Tis the way of the world; 'tis the law of youth, and of unfolding strength. Men are made each with some triumphant superiority, which, through some adaptation of fingers or ear or eye or ciphering or pugilistic or musical or literary craft, enriches the community with a new art; and not only we, but all men of European stock, value these certificates. Giotto could draw a perfect circle: Erwin of Steinbach could build a minster; Olaf, king of Norway, could run round his galley on the blades of the oars of the rowers when the ship was in motion; Ojeda could run out swiftly on a plank projected from the top of a tower, turn round swiftly and come back; Evelyn writes from Rome: "Bernini, the Florentine sculptor, architect, painter and poet, a little before my coming to Rome, gave a public opera, wherein he painted the scenes, cut the statues, invented the engines, composed the music, writ the comedy and built the theatre."

"There is nothing in war," said Napoleon, "which I cannot do by my own hands. If there is nobody to make gunpowder, I can manufacture it. The guncarriages I know how to construct. If it is necessary to make cannons at the forge, I can make them. The details of working them in battle, if it is necessary to teach, I shall teach them. In administration, it is I alone who have arranged the finances, as you know."

It is recorded of Linnaeus, among many proofs of his beneficent skill, that when the timber in the shipyards of Sweden was ruined by rot, Ligneous was desired by the government to find a remedy. He studied the insects that infested the timber, and found that they laid their eggs in the logs within certain days in April, and he directed that during ten days at that season the logs should be immersed under water in the docks; which being done, the timber was found to be uninjured.

Columbus at Veragua found plenty of gold; but leaving the coast, the ship full of one hundred and fifty skillful seamen,—some of them old pilots, and with too much experience of their craft and treachery to him,—the wise admiral kept his private record of his homeward path. And when he reached Spain he told the King and Queen that "they may ask all the pilots who came with him where is Veragua. Let them answer and say if they know where Veragua lies. I assert that they can give no other account than that they went to lands where there was abundance of gold, but they do not know the way to return thither, but would be obliged to go on a voyage of discovery as much as if they had never been there before. There is a mode of reckoning." he proudly adds, "derived from astronomy, which is sure and safe to any one who understands it."

Hippocrates in Greece knew how to stay the devouring plague which ravaged Athens in his time, and his skill died with him. Dr. Benjamin Rush, in Philadelphia, carried that city heroically through the yellow fever of the year 1793. Leverrier carried the Copernican system in his head, and knew where to look for the new planet. We have seen an American woman write a novel of which a million copies were sold, in all languages, and which had one merit, of speaking to the universal heart, and was read with equal interest to three audiences, namely, in the parlor, in the kitchen and in the nursery of every house. [Harriet Beecher Stowe, *Uncle Tom's Cabin*—ed.] We have seen women who could institute hospitals and schools in armies. We have seen a woman who by pure song could melt the souls of whole populations. And there is no limit to these varieties of talent.

These are arts to be thankful for, each one as it is a new direction of human power. We cannot choose but respect them. Our civilization is made up of a million contributions of this kind. For success, to be sure we esteem it a test in other people, since we do first in ourselves. We respect ourselves more if we have succeeded. Neither do we grudge to each of these benefactors the praise or the profit which accrues from his industry.

Here are already quite different degrees of moral merit in these examples. I don't know but we and our race elsewhere set a higher value on wealth, victory and coarse superiority of all kinds, than other men,—have less tranquility of mind, are less easily contented. The Saxon is taught from his infancy to wish to be first. The Norseman was a restless rider, fighter, freebooter. The ancient Norse ballads describe him as afflicted with this inextinguishable thirst of victory. The mother says to her son:

> "Success shall be in thy courser tall,
> Success in thyself, which is best of all,
> Success in thy hand, success in thy foot,
> In struggle with man, in battle with brute:
> The holy God and Saint Drothin dear
> Shall never shut eyes on thy career:
> Look out, look out, Svend Vonved!"

These feats that we extol do not signify so much as we say. These boasted arts are of very recent origin. They are local conveniences, but do not really add to our stature. The greatest men of the world have managed not to want them. Newton was a great man, without telegraph, or gas, or steam-coach, or rubber shoes, or lucifer-matches, or ether for his pain; so was Shakespeare and Alfred and Scipio and Socrates. These are local *conveniences*, but how easy to go now to parts of the world where not only all these arts are wanting, but where they are despised. The Arabian sheiks, the most dignified people in the planet, do not want them; yet have as much self respect as the English, and are easily able to impress the Frenchman or the American who visits them with the respect due to a brave and sufficient man.

These feats have to be sure great difference of merit, and some of them involve power of a high kind. But the public values the invention more than the inventor does. The inventor knows there is much more and better where this came from. The public sees in it a lucrative secret. Men see the reward which the inventor enjoys, and they think, "How shall we win that?" Cause and effect are a little tedious; how to leap to the result by short or by false means? We are not scrupulous. What we ask is victory, without regard to the cause; after the Rob Roy rule, after the Napoleon rule, to be the strongest today, the way of the Talleyrands, prudent people, whose watches go faster than their neighbors', and who detect the first moment of decline and throw themselves on the instant on the winning side. I have heard that Nelson used to say, "Never mind the justice or the impudence, only let me succeed." Lord Brougham's single duty of counsel is, "to get the prisoner clear." Fuller says 'tis a maxim of lawyers that "a crown once worn cleareth all defects of the wearer thereof." *Rien ne reussit mieux que le succes.* And we Americans are tainted with this insanity, as out bankruptcies and our reckless politics may show. We are great by exclusion, grasping and egotism. Our success takes from all what it gives to one, 'tis a haggard, malignant, careworn running for luck.

Egotism is a kind of buckram that gives momentary strength and concentration to men, and seems to be much used in Nature for fabrics in which local and spasmodic energy is required. I could point to men in this country, of indispensable importance to the carrying on of American life, of this humor, whom we could ill spare; any one of them would be a national loss. But it spoils conversation. They will not try conclusions with you. They are ever thrusting this pampered self between you and them. It is plain they have a long education to undergo to reach simplicity and plain-dealing, which are what a wise man mainly cares for in his companion. Nature knows how to convert evil to good: Nature utilizes misers, fanatics, show-men, egotists, to accomplish her ends; but we must not think better of the foible for that. The passion for sudden success is rude and puerile, just as war, cannons and executions are used to clear the ground of bad, lumpish, irreclaimable savages, but always to the damage of the conquerors.

I hate this shallow Americanism which hopes to get rich by credit, to get knowledge by raps on midnight tables. to learn the economy of the mind by phrenology, or skill without study, or mastery without apprenticeship, or the sale of goods through pretending that they sell, or power through making believe you are powerful, or through a packed jury or caucus, bribery and "repeating" votes, or wealth by fraud, They think they have got it, but they have got something else,—a crime which calls for another crime, and another devil behind that: these are steps to suicide, infamy and the harming of mankind. We countenance each other in this life of show, puffing, advertisement and manufacture of public opinion; and excellence is lost sight of in the hunger for sudden performance and praise.

There was a wise man, an Italian artist, Michelangelo, who writes thus of himself: "Meanwhile the Cardinal Ippolito, in whom all my best hopes were placed, being dead, I began to understand that the promises of this world are for the most part vain phantoms, and that to confide in one's self, and become something of worth and value, is the best and safest course." Now, though I am by no means sure that the reader will assent to all my propositions, yet I think we shall agree in my first rule for success,—that we should drop the brag and the advertisement, and take Michelangelo's course, "to confide in one's self, and be something of worth and value."

Each man has an aptitude born with him. Do your work. I have to say this often, but Nature says it oftener. 'Tis clownish to insist on doing all with one's own hands, as if every man should build his own clumsy house, forge his hammer, and bake his dough; but he is to dare to do what he can do best; not help others as they would direct him, but as he knows his helpful power to be. To do otherwise is to neutralize all those extraordinary special talents distributed among men. Yet whilst this self-truth is essential to the exhibition of the world and to the growth and glory of each mind, it is rare to find a man who believes his own thought or who speaks that which he was created to say. As nothing astonishes men so much as common sense and plain dealing, so nothing is more rare in any man than an act of his own. Any work looks wonderful to him, except that which he can do. We do not believe our own thought; we must serve somebody; we must quote somebody; we dote on the old and the distant: we are tickled by great names; we import the religion of other nations; we quote their opinions; we cite their laws. The gravest and learnedest courts in this country shudder to face a new question, and will wait months and years for a case to occur that can be tortured into a precedent, and thus throw on a bolder party the onus of an initiative. Thus we do not carry a counsel in our breasts, or do not know it; and because we cannot shake off from our shoes this dust of Europe and Asia, the world seems to be born old, society is under a spell, every man is a borrower and a mimic, life is theatrical and literature a quotation; and hence that depression of spirits, that furrow of care, said to mark every American brow.

Self-trust is the first secret of success, the belief that if you are here the authorities of the universe put you here, and for cause, or with some task strictly appointed you in your constitution, and so long as you work at that you are well and successful. It by no means consists in rushing prematurely to a showy feat that shall catch the eye and satisfy spectators. It is enough if you work in the right direction. So far from the performance being the real success, it is clear that the success was much earlier than that, namely, when all the feats that make our civility were the thoughts of good heads. The fame of each discovery rightly attaches to the mind that made the formula which contains all the details, and not to the manufacturers who now make their gain by it; although the mob uniformly cheers the publisher, and not the inventor. It is the dulness of the multitude that they cannot see the house in the groundplan; the working, in the model of the projector. Whilst it is a thought, though it were a new fuel, or a new food, or the creation of agriculture, it is cried down, it is a chimera; but when it is a fact, and comes in the shape of eight per cent., ten per cent., a hundred per cent., they cry, "It is the voice of God." Horatio

Greenough the sculptor said to me of Robert Fulton's visit to Paris: "Fulton knocked at the door of Napoleon with steam, and was rejected; and Napoleon lived long enough to know that he had excluded a greater power than his own."

Is there no loving of knowledge, and of art, and of our design, for itself alone? Cannot we please ourselves with performing our work, or gaining truth and power, without being praised for it? I gain my point, I gain all points, if I can reach my companion with any statement which teaches him his own worth. The sum of wisdom is, that the time is never lost that is devoted to work. The good workman never says, "There, that will do;" but, "There, that is it: try it, and come again, it will last always." If the artist, in whatever art, is well at work on his own design, it signifies little that he does not yet find orders or customers. I pronounce that young man happy who is content with having acquired the skill which he had aimed at, and waits willingly when the occasion of making it appreciated shall arrive, knowing well that it will not loiter. The time your rival spends in dressing up his work for effect, hastily, and for the market, you spend in study and experiments towards real knowledge and efficiency. He has thereby sold his picture or machine, or won the prize, or got the appointment; but you have raised yourself into a higher school of art, and a few years will show the advantage of the real master over the short popularity of the showman. I know it is a nice point to discriminate this self-trust, which is the pledge of all mental vigor and performance, from the disease to which it is allied,—the exaggeration of the part which we can play;—yet they are two things. But it is sanity to know that, over my talent or knack. and a million times better than any talent, is the central intelligence which subordinates and uses all talents; and it is only as a door into this, that any talent or the knowledge it gives is of value. He only who comes into this central intelligence, in which no egotism or exaggeration can be, comes into self-possession.

My next point is that in the scale of powers it is not talent but sensibility which is best: talent confines, but the central life puts us in relation to all. How often it seems the chief good to be born with a cheerful temper and well adjusted to the tone of the human race. Such a man feels himself in harmony, and conscious by his receptivity of an infinite strength. Like Alfred, "good fortune accompanies him like a gift of God." Feel yourself, and be not daunted by things. 'Tis the fulness of man that runs over into objects, and makes his Bibles and Shakespeares and Homers so great. The joyful reader borrows of his own ideas to fill their faulty outline, and knows not that he borrows and gives.

There is something of poverty in our criticism. We assume that there are few great men, all the rest are little; that there is but one Homer, but one Shakespeare, one Newton, one Socrates. But the soul in her beaming hour does not acknowledge these usurpations. We should know how to praise Socrates, or Plato, or Saint John, without impoverishing us. In good hours we do not find Shakespeare or Homer over-great, only to have been translators of the happy present, and every man and woman divine possibilities. 'Tis the good reader that makes the good book; a good head cannot read amiss, in every book he finds passages which seem confidences or asides hidden from all else and unmistakably meant for his ear.

The light by which we see in this world comes out from the soul of the observer. Wherever any noble sentiment dwelt, it made the faces and houses around to shine. Nay, the powers of this busy brain are miraculous and illimitable. Therein are the rules and formulas by which the whole empire of matter is worked. There is no prosperity, trade, art, city, or great material wealth of any kind, but if you trace it home, you will find it rooted in a thought of some individual man.

Is all life a surface affair? 'Tis curious, but our difference of wit appears to be only a difference of impressionability, or power to appreciate faint, fainter and infinitely faintest voices and visions. When the scholar or the writer has pumped his brain for thoughts and verses, and then comes abroad into Nature, has he never found that there is a better poetry hinted in a boy's whistle of a tune, or in the piping of a sparrow, than in all his literary results? We call it health. What is so admirable as the health of youth?—with his long days because his eyes are good, and brisk circulations keep him warm in cold rooms, and he loves books that speak to the imagination; and he can read Plato, covered to his chin with a cloak in a cold upper chamber, though he should associate the Dialogues ever after with a woollen smell. 'Tis the bane of life that natural effects are continually crowded out, and artificial arrangements substituted. We remember when in early youth the earth spoke and the heavens glowed; when an evening, any evening, grim and wintry, sleet and snow, was enough for us; the houses were in the air. Now it costs a rare combination of clouds and lights to overcome the common and mean. What is it we look for in the landscape, in sunsets and sunrises, in the sea and the firmament? what but a compensation for the cramp and pettiness of human performances? We bask in the day, and the mind finds somewhat as great as itself. In Nature all is large massive repose. Remember what befalls a city boy who goes for the first time into the October woods. He is suddenly initiated into a pomp and glory that brings to pass for him the dreams of romance. He is the king he dreamed he was; he walks through tents of gold, through bowers of crimson, porphyry and topaz, pavilion on pavilion, garlanded with vines, flowers and sunbeams, with incense and music, with so many hints to his astonished senses; the leaves twinkle and pique and flatter him, and his eye and step are tempted on by what hazy distances to happier solitudes. All this happiness he owes only to his finer perception. The owner of the wood-lot finds only a number of discolored trees, and says, "They ought to come down; they aren't growing any better; they should be cut and corded before spring."

Wordsworth writes of the delights of the boy in Nature;—

> "For never will come back the hour
> Of splendor in the grass, of glory in the flower."

But I have just seen a man, well knowing what he spoke of, who told me that the verse was not true for him; that his eyes opened as he grew older, and that every spring was more beautiful to him than the last.

We live among gods of our own creation. Does that deep-toned bell, which has shortened many a night of ill nerves, render to you nothing but acoustic vibrations? Is the old church which gave you the first lessons of religious life, or the village school, or the college where you first knew the dreams of fancy and joys of thought, only boards or brick and mortar? Is the house in which you were born, or the house in which your dearest friend lived, only a piece of real estate whose value is covered by the Hartford insurance? You walk on the beach and enjoy the animation of the picture. Scoop up a little water in the hollow of your palm, take up a handful of shore sand; well, these are the elements. What is the beach but acres of sand? what is the ocean but cubic miles of water? a little more or less signifies nothing. No, it is that this brute matter is part of somewhat not brute. It is that the sand floor is held by spheral gravity, and bent to be a part of the round globe, under the optical sky,—part of the astonishing astronomy, and existing at last to moral ends and from moral causes.

The world is not made up to the eye of figures, that is, only half; it is also made of color. How that element washes the universe with its enchanting waves! The sculptor had ended his work, and behold a new world of dream-like glory. 'Tis the last stroke of Nature; beyond color she cannot go. In like manner, life is made up, not of knowledge only, but of love also. If thought is form, sentiment is color. It clothes the skeleton world with space, variety and glow. The hues of sunset make life great; so the affections make some little web of cottage and fireside populous, important, and filling the main space in our history.

The fundamental fact in our metaphysic constitution is the correspondence of man to the world, so that every change in that writes a record in the mind. The mind yields sympathetically to the tendencies or law which stream through things and make the order of Nature; and in the perfection of this correspondence or expressiveness, the health and force of man consist. If we follow this hint into our intellectual education, we shall find that it is not propositions, not new dogmas and a logical exposition of the world that are our first need; but to watch and tenderly cherish the intellectual and moral sensibilities, those fountains of right thought, and woo them to stay and make their home with us. Whilst they abide with us we shall not think amiss. Our perception far outruns our talent. We bring a welcome to the highest lessons of religion and of poetry out of all proportion beyond our skill to teach. And, further, the great hearing and sympathy of men is more true and wise than their speaking is wont to be. A deep sympathy is what we require for any student of the mind; for the chief difference between man and man is a difference of impressionability. Aristotle or Bacon or Kant propound some maxim which is the keynote of philosophy thenceforward. But I am more interested to know that when at last they have hurled out their grand word, it is only some familiar experience of every man in the street. If it be not, it will never be heard of again.

Ah! if one could keep this sensibility, and live in the happy sufficing present, and find the day and its cheap means contenting, which only ask receptivity in you, and no strained exertion and cankering ambition, overstimulating to be at the head of your class and the head of society, and to have distinction and laurels and consumption! We are not strong by our power to penetrate, but by our relatedness. The world is enlarged for us, not by new objects, but by finding more affinities and potencies in those we have.

This sensibility appears in the homage to beauty which exalts the faculties of youth; in the power which form and color exert upon the soul; when we see eyes that are a compliment to the human race, features that explain the Phidian sculpture. Fontenelle said: "There are three things about which I have curiosity, though I know nothing of them,—music, poetry and love." The great doctors of this science are the greatest men,— Dante, Petrarch, Michelangelo and Shakespeare. The wise Socrates treats this matter with a certain archness, yet with very marked expressions. "I am always," he says, "asserting that I happen to know, I may say, nothing but a mere trifle relating to matters of love; yet in that kind of learning I lay claim to being more skilled than any one man of the past or present time." They may well speak in this uncertain manner of their knowledge, and in this confident manner of their will, for the secret of it is hard to detect, so deep it is; and yet genius is measured by its skill in this science.

Who is he in youth or in maturity or even in old age, who does not like to hear of those sensibilities which turn curled heads round at church, and send wonderful eye-beams across assemblies, from one to one, never missing in the thickest crowd? The keen statist reckons by tens and hundreds; the genial man is interested in every slipper that comes into the assembly. The passion, alike everywhere, creeps under the snows of Scandinavia, under the fires of the equator, and swims in the seas of Polynesia. Lofn is as puissant a divinity in the Norse Edda as Camadeva in the red vault of India, Eros in the Greek, or Cupid in the Latin heaven. And what is specially true of love is that it is a state of extreme impressionability; the lover has more senses and finer senses than others; his eye and ear are telegraphs; he reads omens on the flower, and cloud, and face, and form, and gesture, and reads them aright. In his surprise at the sudden and entire understanding that is between him and the be loved person, it occurs to him that they might somehow meet independently of time and place. How delicious the belief that he could elude all guards, precautions, ceremonies, means and delays, and hold instant and sempiternal communication! In solitude, in banishment, the hope returned, and the experiment was eagerly tried. The supernal powers seem to take his part. What was on his lips to say is uttered by his friend. When he went abroad, he met, by wonderful casualties, the one person he sought. If in his walk he chanced to look back, his friend was walking behind him. And it has happened that the artist has often drawn in his pictures the face of the future wife whom he had not yet seen.

But also in complacencies nowise so strict as this of the passion, the man of sensibility counts it a delight only to hear a child's voice fully addressed to him, or to see the beautiful manners of the youth of either sex. When the event is past and remote, how insignificant the greatest compared with the piquancy of the present! Today at the school examination the professor interrogates Sylvina in the history class about Odoacer and Alaric. Sylvina can't remember, but suggests that Odoacer was defeated; and the professor tartly replies, "No, he defeated the Romans." But 'tis plain to the visitor that 'tis of no importance at all about Odoacer and 'tis a great deal of importance about Sylvina, and if she says he was defeated, why he had better a great deal have been defeated than give her a moment's annoy. Odoacer, if there was a particle of the gentleman in him, would have said, Let me be defeated a thousand times.

And as our tenderness for youth and beauty gives a new and just importance to their fresh and manifold claims, so the like sensibility gives welcome to all excellence, has eyes and hospitality for merit in corners. An Englishman of marked character and talent, who had brought with him hither one or two friends and a library of mystics, assured me that nobody and nothing of possible interest was left in England, he had brought all that was alive away. I was forced to reply: "No, next door to you probably, on the other side of the partition in the same house, was a greater man than any you had seen." Every man has a history worth knowing, if he could tell it, or if we could draw it from him. Character and wit have their own magnetism. Send a deep man into any town, and he will find another deep man there, unknown hitherto to his neighbors. That is the great happiness of life, to add to our high acquaintances. The very law of averages might have assured you that there will be in every hundred heads, say ten or five good heads. Morals are generated as the atmosphere is. 'Tis a secret, the genesis of either; but the springs of justice and courage do not fail any more than salt or sulphur springs.

The world is always opulent, the oracles are never silent; but the receiver must by a happy temperance be brought to that top of condition, that frolic health, that he can easily take and give these fine communications. Health is the condition of wisdom, and the sign is cheerfulness,— an open and noble temper. There was never poet who had not the heart in the right place. The old trouveur, Pons Capdueil, wrote,—

"Oft have I beard, and deem the witness true,
Whom man delights in, God delights in too."

All beauty warms the heart, is a sign of health, prosperity and the favor of God. Everything lasting and fit for men the Divine Power has marked with this stamp. What delights, what emancipates, not what scars and pains us, is wise and good in speech and in the arts. For, truly, the heart at the centre of the universe with every throb hurls the flood of happiness into every artery, vein and veinlet, so that the whole system is inundated with the tides of joy. The plenty of the poorest place is too great: the harvest cannot be gathered. Every sound ends in music. The edge of every surface is tinged with prismatic rays.

One more trait of true success. The good mind chooses what is positive, what is advancing,—embraces the affirmative. Our system is one of poverty. 'Tis presumed, as I said, there is but one Shakespeare, one Homer, one Jesus,—not that all are or shall be inspired. But we must begin by affirming. Truth and goodness subsist forevermore. It is true there is evil and good, night and day: but these are not equal. The day is great and final. The night is for the day, but the day is not for the night. What is this immortal demand for more, which belongs to our constitution? this enormous ideal? There is no such critic and beggar as this terrible Soul. No historical person begins to content us. We know the satisfactoriness of justice, the sufficiency of truth. We know the answer that leaves nothing to ask. We know the Spirit by its victorious tone. The searching tests to apply to every new pretender are amount and quality,—what does he add? and what is the state of mind he leaves me in? Your theory is unimportant; but what new stock you can add to humanity, or how high you can carry life? A man is a man only as he makes life and nature happier to us.

I fear the popular notion of success stands in direct opposition in all points to the real and wholesome success. One adores public opinion, the other private opinion: one fame, the other desert; one feats, the other humility: one lucre, the other love; one monopoly, and the other hospitality of mind.

We may apply this affirmative law to letters, to manners, to art, to the decorations of our houses, etc. I do not find executions or tortures or lazar-houses, or grisly photographs of the field on the day after the battle, fit subjects for cabinet pictures. I think that some so-called "sacred subjects" must be treated with more genius than I have seen in the masters of Italian or Spanish art to be right pictures for houses and churches. Nature does not invite such exhibition. Nature lays the ground-plan of each creature accurately, sternly fit for all his functions; then veils it scrupulously. See how carefully she covers up the skeleton. The eye shall not see it; the sun shall not shine on it. She weaves her tissues and integuments of flesh and skin and hair and beautiful colors of the day over it, and forces death down underground, and makes haste to cover it up with leaves and vines, and wipes carefully out every trace by new creation. Who and what are you that would lay the ghastly anatomy bare?

Don't hang a dismal picture on the wall, and do not daub with sables and gloomy in your conversation. Don't be a cynic and disconsolate preacher.

Don't bewail and bemoan. Omit the negative propositions. Nerve us with incessant affirmatives. Don't waste yourself in rejection, nor bark against the bad, but chant the beauty of the good. When that is spoken which has a right to be spoken, the chatter and the criticism will stop. Set down nothing that will not help somebody;—

> "For every gift of noble origin
> Is breathed upon by Hope's perpetual breath."

The affirmative of affirmatives is love. As much love, so much perception. As caloric to matter, so is love to mind; so it enlarges, and so it empowers it. Good will makes insight, as one finds his way to the sea by embarking on a river. I have seen scores of people who can silence me, but I seek one who shall make me forget or overcome the frigidities and imbecilities into which I fall. The painter Giotto, Vasari tells us, renewed art because he put more goodness into his heads. To awake in man and to raise the sense of worth, to educate his feeling and judgment so that he shall scorn himself for a bad action, that is the only aim.

'Tis cheap and easy to destroy. There is not a joyful boy or an innocent girl buoyant with fine purposes of duty, in all the street full of eager and rosy faces, but a cynic can chill and dishearten with a single word. Despondency comes readily enough to the most sanguine. The cynic has only to follow their hint with his bitter confirmation, and they check that eager courageous pace and go home with heavier step and premature age. They will themselves quickly enough give the hint he wants to the cold wretch. Which of them has not failed to please where they most wished it, or blundered where they were most ambitious of success? or found themselves awkward or tedious or incapable of study, thought or heroism, and only hoped by good sense and fidelity to do what they could and pass unblamed? And this witty malefactor makes their little hope less with satire and skepticism, and slackens the springs of endeavor. Yes, this is easy; but to help the young soul, add energy, inspire hope and blow the coals into a useful flame; to redeem defeat by new thought, by firm action, that is not easy, that is the work of divine men.

We live on different planes or platforms. There is an external life, which is educated at school, taught to read, write, cipher and trade; taught to grasp all the boy can get, urging him to put himself forward, to make himself useful and agreeable in the world, to ride, run, argue and contend, unfold his talents, shine, conquer and possess.

But the inner life sits at home, and does not learn to do things, nor value these feats at all. 'Tis a quiet, wise perception. It loves truth, because it is itself real: it loves right, it knows nothing else; but it makes no progress; was as wise in our first memory of it as now; is just the same now in maturity and hereafter in age, it was in youth. We have grown to manhood and womanhood; we have powers, connection, children, reputations, professions: this makes no account of them all. It lives in the great present; it makes the present great. This tranquil, well-founded, wide-seeing soul is no express-rider, no attorney, no magistrate: it lies in the sun and broods on the world. A person of this temper once said to a man of much activity, "I will pardon you that you do so much, and you me that I do nothing." And Euripides says that "Zeus hates busybodies and those who do too much."

Emerson's Keys to Success

Excellence is lost sight of in the hunger for sudden performance and praise.

We should drop the brag and the advertisement, and take Michelangelo's course, "to confide in one's self, and be something of worth and value."

Self-trust is the first secret of success.

The sum of wisdom is, that the time is never lost that is devoted to work.

We are not strong by our power to penetrate, but by our relatedness.

*There is no prosperity, trade, art, city,
or great material wealth of any kind, but if you trace it home,
you will find it rooted in a thought of some individual man.*

*Every man has a history worth knowing, if he could tell it,
or if we could draw it from him.*

*Health is the condition of wisdom, and the sign is cheerfulness,—
an open and noble temper.*

*The good mind chooses what is positive, what is advancing,—
embraces the affirmative.*

*Don't waste yourself in rejection, nor bark against the bad,
but chant the beauty of the good.*

The affirmative of affirmatives is love.

Power

> His tongue was framed to music,
> And his hand was armed with skill,
> His face was the mould of beauty,
> And his heart the throne of will.

THERE IS NOT YET ANY INVENTORY of a man's faculties, any more than a bible of his opinions. Who shall set a limit to the influence of a human being? There are men, who, by their sympathetic attractions, carry nations with them, and lead the activity of the human race. And if there be such a tie, that, wherever the mind of man goes, nature will accompany him, perhaps there are men whose magnetisms are of that force to draw material and elemental powers, and, where they appear, immense instrumentalities organize around them. Life is a search after power; and this is an element with which the world is so saturated,—there is no chink or crevice in which it is not lodged,—that no honest seeking goes unrewarded. A man should prize events and possessions as the ore in which this fine mineral is found; and he can well afford to let events and possessions, and the breath of the body go, if their value has been added to him in the shape of power. If he have secured the elixir, he can spare the wide gardens from which it was distilled. A cultivated man, wise to know and bold to perform, is the end to which nature works, and the education of the will is the flowering and result of all this geology and astronomy.

All successful men have agreed in one thing,—they were *causationists*. They believed that things went not by luck, but by law; that there was not a weak or a cracked link in the chain that joins the first and last of things. A belief in causality, or strict connection between every trifle and the principle of being, and, in consequence, belief in compensation, or, that nothing is got for nothing,—characterizes all valuable minds, and must control every effort that is made by an industrious one. The most valiant men are the best believers in the tension of the laws. "All the great captains," said Bonaparte, "have performed vast achievements by conforming with the rules of the art,—by adjusting efforts to obstacles."

The key to the age may be this, or that, or the other, as the young orators describe;—the key to all ages is—Imbecility; imbecility in the vast majority of men, at all times, and, even in heroes, in all but certain eminent moments; victims of gravity, custom, and fear. This gives force to the strong,—that the multitude have no habit of self-reliance or original action.

We must reckon success a constitutional trait. Courage,—the old physicians taught, (and their meaning holds, if their physiology is a little mythical),—courage, or the degree of life, is as the degree of circulation of the blood in the arteries. "During passion, anger, fury, trials of strength, wrestling, fighting, a large amount of blood is collected in the arteries, the maintenance of bodily strength requiring it, and but little is sent into the veins. This condition is constant with intrepid persons." Where the arteries hold their blood, is courage and adventure possible. Where they pour it unrestrained into the veins, the spirit is low and feeble. For performance of great mark, it needs extraordinary health. If Eric is in robust health, and has slept well, and is at the top of his condition, and thirty years old, at his departure from Greenland, he will steer west, and his ships will reach Newfoundland. But take out Eric, and put in a stronger and bolder man,—Biorn, or Thorfin,—and the ships will, with just as much ease, sail six hundred, one thousand, fifteen hundred miles further, and reach Labrador and New England. There is no chance in results. With adults, as with children, one class enter cordially into the game, and whirl with the whirling world; the others have cold hands, and remain bystanders; or are only dragged in by the humor and vivacity of those who can carry a dead weight. The first wealth is health. Sickness is poor-spirited, and cannot serve any one: it must husband its resources to live. But health or fulness answers its own ends, and has to spare, runs over, and inundates the neighborhoods and creeks of other men's necessities.

All power is of one kind, a sharing of the nature of the world. The mind that is parallel with the laws of nature will be in the current of events, and strong with their strength. One man is made of the same stuff of which events are made; is in sympathy with the course of things; can predict it. Whatever befalls, befalls him first; so that he is equal to whatever shall happen. A man who knows men, can talk well on politics, trade, law, war, religion. For, everywhere, men are led in the same manners.

The advantage of a strong pulse is not to be supplied by any labor, art, or concert. It is like the climate, which easily rears a crop, which no glass, or irrigation, or tillage, or manures, can elsewhere rival. It is like the opportunity of a city like New York, or Constantinople, which needs no diplomacy to force capital or genius or labor to it. They come of themselves, as the waters flow to it. So a broad, healthy, massive understanding seems to lie on the shore of unseen rivers, of unseen oceans, which are covered with barks, that, night and day, are drifted to this point. That is poured into its lap, which other men lie plotting for. It is in everybody's secret; anticipates everybody's discovery; and if it do not command every fact of the genius and the scholar, it is because it is large and sluggish, and does not think them worth the exertion which you do.

This affirmative force is in one, and is not in another, as one horse has the spring in him, and another in the whip. "On the neck of the young man," said Hafiz, "sparkles no gem so gracious as enterprise." Import into any stationary district, as into an old Dutch population in New York or Pennsylvania, or among the planters of Virginia, a colony of hardy Yankees, with seething brains, heads full of steam-hammer, pulley, crank, and toothed wheel,—and everything begins to shine with values. What enhancement to all the water and land in England, is the arrival of James Watt or Brunel! In every company, there is not only the active and passive sex, but, in both men and women, a deeper and more important *sex of mind*, namely, the inventive or creative class of both men and women, and the uninventive or accepting class. Each plus man represents his set, and, if he have the accidental advantage of personal ascendency,—which implies neither more nor less of talent, but merely the temperamental or taming eye of a soldier or a schoolmaster, (which one has, and one has not, as one has a black mustache and one a blond,) then quite easily and without envy or resistance, all his coadjutors and feeders will admit his right to absorb them. The merchant works by book-keeper and cashier; the lawyer's authorities are hunted up by clerks; the geologist reports the surveys of his subalterns; Commander Wilkes appropriates the results of all the naturalists attached to the Expedition; Thorwaldsen's statue is finished by stone-cutters; Dumas has journeymen; and Shakespeare was theatre-manager, and used the labor of many young men, as well as the playbooks.

There is always room for a man of force, and he makes room for many. Society is a troop of thinkers, and the best heads among them take the best places. A feeble man can see the farms that are fenced and tilled, the houses that are built. The strong man sees the possible houses and farms. His eye makes estates, as fast as the sun breeds clouds.

When a new boy comes into school, when a man travels, and encounters strangers every day, or, when into any old club a new comer is domesticated, that happens which befalls, when a strange ox is driven into a pen or pasture where cattle are kept; there is at once a trial of strength between the best pair of horns and the new comer, and it is settled thenceforth which is the leader. So now, there is a measuring of strength, very courteous, but decisive, and an acquiescence thenceforward when these two meet. Each reads his fate in the other's eyes. The weaker party finds, that none of his information or wit quite fits the occasion. He thought he knew this or that: he finds that he omitted to learn the end of it. Nothing that he knows will quite hit the mark, whilst all the rival's arrows are good, and well thrown. But if he knew all the facts in the encyclopedia, it would not help him: for this is an affair of presence of mind, of attitude, of aplomb: the opponent has the sun and wind, and, in every cast, the choice of weapon and mark; and, when he himself is matched with some other antagonist, his own shafts fly well and hit. 'Tis a question of stomach and constitution. The second man is as good as the first,—perhaps better; but has not stoutness or stomach, as the first has, and so his wit seems over-fine or under-fine.

Health is good,—power, life, that resists disease, poison, and all enemies, and is conservative, as well as creative. Here is question, every spring, whether to graft with wax, or whether with clay; whether to whitewash or to potash, or to prune; but the one point is the thrifty tree. A good tree, that agrees with the soil, will grow in spite of blight, or bug, or pruning, or neglect, by night and by day, in all weathers and all treatments. Vivacity, leadership, must be had, and we are not allowed to be nice in choosing. We must fetch the pump with dirty water, if clean cannot be had. If we will make bread, we must have contagion, yeast, emptyings, or what not, to induce fermentation into the dough: as the torpid artist seeks inspiration at any cost, by virtue or by vice, by friend or by fiend, by prayer or by wine. And we have a certain instinct, that where is great amount of life, though gross and peccant, it has its own checks and purifications, and will be found at last in harmony with moral laws.

We watch in children with pathetic interest, the degree in which they possess recuperative force. When they are hurt by us, or by each other, or go to the bottom of the class, or miss the annual prizes, or are beaten in the game,—if they lose heart, and remember the mischance in their chamber at home, they have a serious check. But if they have the buoyancy and resistance that preoccupies them with new interest in the new moment,—the wounds cicatrize, and the fibre is the tougher for the hurt.

One comes to value this plus health, when he sees that all difficulties vanish before it. A timid man listening to the alarmists in Congress, and in the newspapers, and observing the profligacy of party,—sectional interests urged with a fury which shuts its eyes to consequences, with a mind made up to desperate extremities, ballot in one hand, and rifle in the other,—might easily believe that he and his country have seen their best days, and he hardens himself the best he can against the coming ruin. But, after this has been foretold with equal confidence fifty times, and government six per cents have not declined a quarter of a mill, he discovers that the enormous elements of strength which are here in play, make our politics unimportant.

Personal power, freedom, and the resources of nature strain every faculty of every citizen. We prosper with such vigor, that, like thrifty trees, which grow in spite of ice, lice, mice, and borers, so we do not suffer from the profligate swarms that fatten on the national treasury. The huge animals nourish huge parasites, and the rancor of the disease attests the strength of the constitution. The same energy in the Greek Demos drew the remark, that the evils of popular government appear greater than they are; there is compensation for them in the spirit and energy it awakens. The rough and ready style which belongs to a people of sailors, foresters, farmers, and mechanics, has its advantages. Power educates the potentate. As long as our people quote English standards they dwarf their own proportions. A Western lawyer of eminence said to me he wished it were a penal offense to bring an English law-book into a court in this country, so pernicious had he found in his experience our deference to English precedent. The very word 'commerce' has only an English meaning, and is pinched to the cramp exigencies of English experience. The commerce of rivers, the commerce of railroads, and who knows but the commerce of air-balloons, must add an American extension to the pond-hole of admiralty. As long as our people quote English standards, they will miss the sovereignty of power; but let these rough riders,—legislators in shirt-sleeves,—Hoosier, Sucker, Wolverine, Badger,—or whatever hard head Arkansas, Oregon, or Utah sends, half orator, half assassin, to represent its wrath and cupidity at Washington,—let these drive as they may; and the disposition of territories and public lands, the necessity of balancing and keeping at bay the snarling majorities of German, Irish, and of native millions, will bestow promptness, address, and reason, at last, on our buffalo-hunter, and authority and majesty of manners. The instinct of the people is right. Men expect from good whigs, put into office by the respectability of the country, much less skill to deal with Mexico, Spain, Britain, or with our own malcontent members, than from some strong transgressor, like Jefferson, or Jackson, who first conquers his own government, and then uses the same genius to conquer the foreigner. The senators who dissented from Mr. Polk's Mexican war, were not those who knew better, but those who, from political position, could afford it; not Webster, but Benton and Calhoun.

This power, to be sure, is not clothed in satin. 'Tis the power of Lynch law, of soldiers and pirates; and it bullies the peaceable and loyal. But it brings its own antidote; and here is my point,—that all kinds of power usually emerge at the same time; good energy, and bad; power of mind, with physical health; the ecstasies of devotion, with the exasperations of debauchery. The same elements are always present, only sometimes these conspicuous, and sometimes those; what was yesterday foreground, being to-day background,—what was surface, playing now a not less effective part as basis. The longer the drought lasts, the more is the atmosphere surcharged with water. The faster the ball falls to the sun, the force to fly off is by so much augmented. And, in morals, wild liberty breeds iron conscience; natures with great impulses have great resources, and return from far. In politics, the sons of democrats will be whigs; whilst red republicanism, in the father, is a spasm of nature to engender an intolerable tyrant in the next age. On the other hand, conservatism, ever more timorous and narrow, disgusts the children, and drives them for a mouthful of fresh air into radicalism.

Those who have most of this coarse energy,—the 'bruisers,' who have run the gauntlet of caucus and tavern through the county or the state, have their own vices, but they have the good nature of strength and courage. Fierce and unscrupulous, they are usually frank and direct, and above falsehood. Our politics fall into bad hands, and churchmen and men of refinement, it seems agreed, are not fit persons to send to Congress. Politics is a deleterious profession, like some poisonous handicrafts. Men in power have no opinions, but may be had cheap for any opinion, for any purpose,—and if it be only a question between the most civil and the most forcible, I lean to the last. These Hoosiers and Suckers are really better than the sniveling opposition. Their wrath is at least of a bold and manly cast. They see, against the unanimous declarations of the people, how much crime the people will bear; they proceed from step to step, and they have calculated but too justly upon their Excellencies, the New England governors, and upon their Honors, the New England legislators. The messages of the governors and the resolutions of the legislatures, are a proverb for expressing a sham virtuous indignation, which, in the course of events, is sure to be belied.

In trade, also, this energy usually carries a trace of ferocity. Philanthropic and religious bodies do not commonly make their executive officers out of saints. The communities hitherto founded by Socialists,—the Jesuits, the Port-Royalists, the American communities at New Harmony, at Brook Farm, at Zoar, are only possible, by installing Judas as steward. The rest of the offices may be filled by good burgesses. The pious and charitable proprietor has a foreman not quite so pious and charitable. The most amiable of country gentlemen has a certain pleasure in the teeth of the bull-dog which guards his orchard. Of the Shaker society, it was formerly a sort of proverb in the country, that they always sent the devil to market. And in representations of the Deity, painting, poetry, and popular religion have ever drawn the wrath from Hell. It is an esoteric doctrine of society, that a little wickedness is good to make muscle; as if conscience were not good for hands and legs, as if poor decayed formalists of law and order cannot run like wild goats, wolves, and conies; that, as there is a use in medicine for poisons, so the world cannot move without rogues; that public spirit and the ready hand are as well found among the malignants. 'Tis not very rare, the coincidence of sharp private and political practice, with public spirit, and good neighborhood.

I knew a burly Boniface who for many years kept a public-house in one of our rural capitals. He was a knave whom the town could ill spare. He was a social, vascular creature, grasping and selfish. There was no crime which he did not or could not commit. But he made good friends of the selectmen, served them with his best chop, when they supped at his house, and also with his honor the Judge, he was very cordial, grasping his hand. He introduced all the fiends, male and female, into the town, and united in his person the functions of bully, incendiary, swindler, barkeeper, and burglar. He girdled the trees, and cut off the horses' tails of the temperance people, in the night. He led the 'rummies' and radicals in town-meeting with a speech. Meantime, he was civil, fat, and easy, in his house, and precisely the most public-spirited citizen. He was active in getting the roads repaired and planted with shade-trees; he subscribed for the fountains, the gas, and the telegraph; he introduced the new horse-rake, the new scraper, the baby-jumper, and what not, that Connecticut sends to the admiring citizens. He did this the easier, that the peddler stopped at his house, and paid his keeping, by setting up his new trap on the landlord's premises.

Whilst thus the energy for originating and executing work, deforms itself by excess, and so our axe chops off our own fingers,—this evil is not without remedy. All the elements whose aid man calls in, will sometimes become his masters, especially those of most subtle force. Shall he, then, renounce steam, fire, and electricity, or, shall he learn to deal with them? The rule for this whole class of agencies is,—all *plus* is good; only put it in the right place.

Men of this surcharge of arterial blood cannot live on nuts, herb-tea, and elegies; cannot read novels, and play whist; cannot satisfy all their wants at the Thursday Lecture, or the Boston Athenaeum. They pine for adventure, and must go to Pike's Peak; had rather die by the hatchet of a Pawnee, than sit all day and every day at a counting-room desk. They are made for war, for the sea, for mining, hunting, and clearing; for hair-breadth adventures, huge risks, and the joy of eventful living. Some men cannot endure an hour of calm at sea. I remember a poor Malay cook, on board a Liverpool packet, who, when the wind blew a gale, could not contain his joy; "Blow!" he cried, "me do tell you, blow!" Their friends and governors must see that some vent for their explosive complexion is provided. The roisters who are destined for infamy at home, if sent to Mexico, will "cover you with glory," and come back heroes and generals. There are Oregons, Californias, and Exploring Expeditions enough appertaining to America, to find them in files to gnaw, and in crocodiles to eat. The young English are fine animals, full of blood, and when they have no wars to breathe their riotous valors in, they seek for travels as dangerous as war, diving into Maelstroms; swimming Hellesponts; wading up the snowy Himmaleh; hunting lion, rhinoceros, elephant, in South Africa; gypsying with Borrow in Spain and Algiers; riding alligators in South America with Waterton; utilizing Bedouin, Sheik, and Pacha, with Layard; yachting among the icebergs of Lancaster Sound; peeping into craters on the equator; or running on the creases of Malays in Borneo.

The excess of virility has the same importance in general history, as in private and industrial life. Strong race or strong individual rests at last on natural forces, which are best in the savage, who, like the beasts around him, is still in reception of the milk from the teats of Nature. Cut off the connection between any of our works, and this aboriginal source, and the work is shallow. The people lean on this, and the mob is not quite so bad an argument as we sometimes say, for it has this good side. "March without the people," said a French deputy from the tribune, "and you march into night: their instincts are a finger-pointing of Providence, always turned toward real benefit. But when you espouse an Orleans party, or a Bourbon, or a Montalembert party, or any other but an organic party, though you mean well, you have a personality instead of a principle, which will inevitably drag you into a corner."

The best anecdotes of this force are to be had from savage life, in explorers, soldiers, and buccaneers. But who cares for fallings-out of assassins, and fights of bears, or grindings of icebergs? Physical force has no value, where there is nothing else. Snow in snow-banks, fire in volcanoes and solfataras is cheap. The luxury of ice is in tropical countries, and midsummer days. The luxury of fire is, to have a little on our hearth: and of electricity, not volleys of the charged cloud, but the manageable stream on the battery-wires. So of spirit, or energy; the rests or remains of it in the civil and moral man, are worth all the cannibals in the Pacific.

In history, the great moment is, when the savage is just ceasing to be a savage, with all his hairy Pelasgic strength directed on his opening sense of beauty:—and you have Pericles and Phidias,—not yet passed over into the Corinthian civility. Everything good in nature and the world is in that moment of transition, when the swarthy juices still flow plentifully from nature, but their astringency or acridity is got out by ethics and humanity.

The triumphs of peace have been in some proximity to war. Whilst the hand was still familiar with the sword-hilt, whilst the habits of the camp were still visible in the port and complexion of the gentleman, his intellectual power culminated: the compression and tension of these stern conditions is a training for the finest and softest arts, and can rarely be compensated in tranquil times, except by some analogous vigor drawn from occupations as hardy as war.

We say that success is constitutional; depends on a *plus* condition of mind and body, on power of work, on courage; that it is of main efficacy in carrying on the world, and, though rarely found in the right state for an article of commerce, but oftener in the supersaturate or excess, which makes it dangerous and destructive, yet it cannot be spared, and must be had in that form, and absorbents provided to take off its edge.

The affirmative class monopolize the homage of mankind. They originate and execute all the great feats. What a force was coiled up in the skull of Napoleon! Of the sixty thousand men making his army at Eylau, it seems some thirty thousand were thieves and burglars. The men whom, in peaceful communities, we hold if we can, with iron at their legs, in prisons, under the muskets of sentinels, this man dealt with, hand to hand, dragged them to their duty, and won his victories by their bayonets.

This aboriginal might gives a surprising pleasure when it appears under conditions of supreme refinement, as in the proficients in high art. When Michelangelo was forced to paint the Sistine Chapel in fresco, of which art he knew nothing, he went down into the Pope's gardens behind the Vatican, and with a shovel dug out ochres, red and yellow, mixed them with glue and water with his own hands, and having, after many trials, at last suited himself, climbed his ladders, and painted away, week after week, month after month, the sibyls and prophets. He surpassed his successors in rough vigor, as much as in purity of intellect and refinement. He was not crushed by his one picture left unfinished at last. Michel was wont to draw his figures first in skeleton, then to clothe them with flesh, and lastly to drape them. "Ah!" said a brave painter to me, thinking on these things, "if a man has failed, you will find he has dreamed instead of working. There is no way to success in our art, but to take off your coat, grind paint, and work like a digger on the railroad, all day and every day."

Success goes thus invariably with a certain *plus* or positive power: an ounce of power must balance an ounce of weight. And, though a man cannot return into his mother's womb, and be born with new amounts of vivacity, yet there are two economies, which are the best succedanea which the case admits. The first is, the stopping off decisively our miscellaneous activity, and concentrating our force on one or a few points; as the gardener, by severe pruning, forces the sap of the tree into one or two vigorous limbs, instead of suffering it to spindle into a sheaf of twigs.

"Enlarge not thy destiny," said the oracle: "endeavor not to do more than is given thee in charge." The one prudence in life is concentration; the one evil is dissipation: and it makes no difference whether our dissipations are coarse or fine; property and its cares, friends, and a social habit, or politics, or music, or feasting. Everything is good which takes away one plaything and delusion more, and drives us home to add one stroke of faithful work. Friends, books, pictures, lower duties, talents, flatteries, hopes,—all are distractions which cause oscillations in our giddy balloon, and make a good poise and a straight course impossible. You must elect your work; you shall take what your brain can, and drop all the rest. Only so, can that amount of vital force accumulate, which can make the step from knowing to doing. No matter how much faculty of idle seeing a man has, the step from knowing to doing is rarely taken. 'Tis a step out of a chalk circle of imbecility into fruitfulness. Many an artist lacking this, lacks all: he sees the masculine Angelo or Cellini with despair. He, too, is up to Nature and the First Cause in his thought. But the spasm to collect and swing his whole being into one act, he has not. The poet Campbell said, that "a man accustomed to work was equal to any achievement he resolved on, and, that, for himself, necessity not inspiration was the prompter of his muse."

Concentration is the secret of strength in politics, in war, in trade, in short, in all management of human affairs. One of the high anecdotes of the world is the reply of Newton to the inquiry, "how he had been able to achieve his discoveries?"—"By always intending my mind." Or if you will have a text from politics, take this from Plutarch: "There was, in the whole city, but one street in which Pericles was ever seen, the street which led to the market-place and the council house. He declined all invitations to banquets, and all gay assemblies and company. During the whole period of his administration, he never dined at the table of a friend." Or if we seek an example from trade,—"I hope," said a good man to Rothyschild, "your children are not too fond of money and business: I am sure you would not wish that."—"I am sure I should wish that: I wish them to give mind, soul, heart, and body to business,—that is the way to be happy. It requires a great deal of boldness and a great deal of caution, to make a great fortune, and when you have got it, it requires ten times as much wit to keep it. If I were to listen to all the projects proposed to me, I should ruin myself very soon. Stick to one business, young man. Stick to your brewery, (he said this to young Buxton,) and you will be the great brewer of London. Be brewer, and banker, and merchant, and manufacturer, and you will soon be in the Gazette."

Many men are knowing, many are apprehensive and tenacious, but they do not rush to a decision. But in our flowing affairs a decision must be made,—the best, if you can; but any is better than none. There are twenty ways of going to a point, and one is the shortest; but set out at once on one. A man who has that presence of mind which can bring to him on the instant all he knows, is worth for action a dozen men who know as much, but can only bring it to light slowly. The good Speaker in the House is not the man who knows the theory of parliamentary tactics, but the man who decides off-hand. The good judge is not he who does hair-splitting justice to every allegation, but who, aiming at substantial justice, rules something intelligible for the guidance of suitors. The good lawyer is not the man who has an eye to every side and angle of contingency, and qualifies all his qualifications, but who throws himself on your part so heartily, that he can get you out of a scrape. Dr. Johnson said, in one of his flowing sentences, "Miserable beyond all names of wretchedness is that unhappy pair, who are doomed to reduce beforehand to the principles of abstract reason all the details of each domestic day. There are cases where little can be said, and much must be done."

The second substitute for temperament is drill, the power of use and routine. The hack is a better roadster than the Arab barb. In chemistry, the galvanic stream, slow, but continuous, is equal in power to the electric spark, and is, in our arts, a better agent. So in human action, against the spasm of energy, we offset the continuity of drill. We spread the same amount of force over much time, instead of condensing it into a moment. 'Tis the same ounce of gold here in a ball, and there in a leaf. At West Point, Col. Buford, the chief engineer, pounded with a hammer on the trunnions of a cannon, until he broke them off. He fired a piece of ordnance some hundred times in swift succession, until it burst. Now which stroke broke the trunnion? Every stroke. Which blast burst the piece? Every blast. "*Diligence passe sens,*" Henry VIII was wont to say, or, great is drill. John Kemble said, that the worst provincial company of actors would go through a play better than the best amateur company. Basil Hall likes to show that the worst regular troops will beat the best volunteers. Practice is nine tenths. A course of mobs is good practice for orators. All the great speakers were bad speakers at first. Stumping it through England for seven years, made Cobden a consummate debater. Stumping it through New England for twice seven, trained Wendell Phillips. The way to learn German, is, to read the same dozen pages over and over a hundred times, till you know every word and particle in them, and can pronounce and repeat them by heart. No genius can recite a ballad at first reading, so well as mediocrity can at the fifteenth or twentieth readying. The rule for hospitality and Irish 'help,' is, to have the same dinner every day throughout the year. At last, Mrs. O'Shaughnessy learns to cook it to a nicety, the host learns to carve it, and the guests are well served. A humorous friend of mine thinks, that the reason why Nature is so perfect in her art, and gets up such inconceivably fine sunsets, is, that she has learned how, at last, by dint of doing the same thing so very often. Cannot one converse better on a topic on which he has experience, than on one which is new? Men whose opinion is valued on exchange, are only such as have a special experience, and off that ground their opinion is not valuable. "More are made good by exercise, rather than by nature," said Democritus. The friction in nature is so enormous that we cannot spare any power. It is not question to express our thought, to elect our way, but to overcome resistances of the medium and material in everything we do. Hence the use of drill, and the worthlessness of amateurs to cope with practitioners. Six hours every day at the piano, only to give facility of touch; six hours a day at painting, only to give command of the odious materials, oil, ochres, and brushes. The masters say, that they know a master in music, only by seeing the pose of the hands on the keys;—so difficult and vital an act is the command of the instrument. To have learned the use of the tools, by thousands of manipulations; to have learned the arts of reckoning, by endless adding and dividing, is the power of the mechanic and the clerk.

I remarked in England, in confirmation of a frequent experience at home, that, in literary circles, the men of trust and consideration, bookmakers, editors, university deans and professors, bishops, too, were by no means men of the largest literary talent, but usually of a low and ordinary intellectuality, with a sort of mercantile activity and working talent. Indifferent hacks and mediocrities tower, by pushing their forces to a lucrative point, or by working power, over multitudes of superior men, in Old as in New England.

I have not forgotten that there are sublime considerations which limit the value of talent and superficial success. We can easily overpraise the vulgar hero. There are sources on which we have not drawn. I know what I abstain from. But this force or spirit, being the means relied on by Nature for bringing the work of the day about,—as far as we attach importance to household life, and the prizes of the world, we must respect that. And I hold, that an economy may be applied to it; it is as much a subject of exact law and arithmetic as fluids and gases are; it may be husbanded, or wasted; every man is efficient only as he is a container or vessel of this force, and never was any signal act or achievement in history, but by this expenditure. This is not gold, but the gold-maker; not the fame, but the exploit.

If these forces and this husbandry are within reach of our will, and the laws of them can be read, we infer that all success, and all conceivable benefit for man, is also, first or last, within his reach, and has its own sublime economies by which it may be attained. The world is mathematical, and has no casualty, in all its vast and flowing curve. Success has no more eccentricity, than the gingham and muslin we weave in our mills. I know no more affecting lesson to our busy, plotting New England brains, than to go into one of the factories with which we have lined all the watercourses in the States. A man hardly knows how much he is a machine, until he begins to make telegraph, loom, press, and locomotive, in his own image. But in these, he is forced to leave out his follies and hindrances, so that when we go to the mill, the machine is more moral than we. Let a man dare go to a loom, and see if he be equal to it. Let machine confront machine, and see how they come out. The world-mill is more complex than the calico-mill, and the architect stooped less. In the gingham-mill, a broken thread or a shred spoils the web through a piece of a hundred yards, and is traced back to the girl that wove it, and lessens her wages. The stockholder, on being shown this, rubs his hands with delight. Are you so cunning, Mr. Profitloss, and do you expect to swindle *your* master and employer, in the web you weave? A day is a more magnificent cloth than any muslin, the mechanism that makes it is infinitely cunninger, and you shall not conceal the sleazy, fraudulent, rotten hours you have slipped into the piece, nor fear that any honest thread, or straighter steel, or more inflexible shaft, will not testify in the web.

Emerson's Keys to Success

All successful men have agreed in one thing,—they were causationists. They believed that things went not by luck, but by law.

All power is of one kind, a sharing of the nature of the world.

The mind that is parallel with the laws of nature will be in the current of events, and strong with their strength.

There is always room for a man of force, and he makes room for many.

A feeble man can see the farms that are fenced and tilled, the houses that are built. The strong man sees the possible houses and farms.

The evils of popular government appear greater than they are; there is compensation for them in the spirit and energy it awakens.

The rough and ready style which belongs to a people of sailors, foresters, farmers, and mechanics, has its advantages.

Cut off the connection between any of our works, and this aboriginal source [Nature], and the work is shallow.

The affirmative class monopolize the homage of mankind. They originate and execute all the great feats.

Success goes thus invariably with a certain plus *or positive power.*

Concentration is the secret of strength in politics, in war, in trade, in short, in all management of human affairs.

All success, and all conceivable benefit for man, is also, first or last, within his reach.

Wealth

As soon as a stranger is introduced into any company, one of the first questions which all wish to have answered, is, How does that man get his living? And with reason. He is no whole man until he knows how to earn a blameless livelihood. Society is barbarous, until every industrious man can get his living without dishonest customs.

Every man is a consumer, and ought to be a producer. He fails to make his place good in the world, unless he not only pays his debt, but also adds something to the common wealth. Nor can he do justice to his genius, without making some larger demand on the world than a bare subsistence. He is by constitution expensive, and needs to be rich.

Wealth has its source in applications of the mind to nature, from the rudest strokes of spade and axe, up to the last secrets of art. Intimate ties subsist between thought and all production; because a better order is equivalent to vast amounts of brute labor. The forces and the resistances are Nature's, but the mind acts in bringing things from where they abound to where they are wanted; in wise combining; in directing the practice of the useful arts, and in the creation of finer values, by fine art, by eloquence, by song, or the reproductions of memory. Wealth is in applications of mind to nature; and the art of getting rich consists not in industry, much less in saving, but in a better order, in timeliness, in being at the right spot. One man has stronger arms, or longer legs; another sees by the course of streams, and growth of markets, where land will be wanted, makes a clearing to the river, goes to sleep, wakes up rich. Steam is no stronger now, than it was a hundred years ago; but is put to better use. A clever fellow was acquainted with the expansive force of steam; he also saw the wealth of wheat and grass rotting in Michigan. Then he cunningly screws on the steam-pipe to the wheat-crop. Puff now, O Steam! The steam puffs and expands as before, but this time it is dragging all Michigan at its back to hungry New York and hungry England. Coal lay in ledges under the ground since the Flood, until a laborer with pick and windlass brings it to the surface. We may well call it black diamonds. Every basket is power and civilization. For coal is a portable climate. It carries the heat of the tropics to Labrador and the polar circle: and it is the means of transporting itself whithersoever it is wanted. Watt and Stephenson whispered in the ear of mankind their secret, that a *half-ounce of coal will draw two tons a mile*, and coal carries coal, by rail and by boat, to make Canada as warm as Calcutta, and with its comfort brings its industrial power.

When the farmer's peaches are taken from under the tree, and carried into town, they have a new look, and a hundredfold value over the fruit which grew on the same bough, and lies fulsomely on the ground. The craft of the merchant is this bringing a thing from where it abounds, to where it is costly.

Wealth begins in a tight roof that keeps the rain and wind out; in a good pump that yields you plenty of sweet water; in two suits of clothes, so to change your dress when you are wet; in dry sticks to burn; in a good double-wick lamp; and three meals; in a horse, or a locomotive, to cross the land; in a boat to cross the sea; in tools to work with; in books to read; and so, in giving, on all sides, by tools and auxiliaries, the greatest possible extension to our powers, as if it added feet, and hands, and eyes, and blood, length to the day, and knowledge, and good-will.

Wealth begins with these articles of necessity. And here we must recite the iron law which Nature thunders in these northern climates. First, she requires that each man should feed himself. If, happily, his fathers have left him no inheritance, he must go to work, and by making his wants less, or his gains more, he must draw himself out of that state of pain and insult in which she forces the beggar to lie. She gives him no rest until this is done: she starves, taunts, and torments him, takes away warmth, laughter, sleep, friends, and daylight, until he has fought his way to his own loaf. Then, less peremptorily, but still with sting enough, she urges him to the acquisition of such things as belong to him. Every warehouse and shop-window, every fruit-tree, every thought of every hour, opens a new want to him, which it concerns his power and dignity to gratify. It is of no use to argue the wants down: the philosophers have laid the greatness of man in making his wants few; but will a man content himself with a hut and a handful of dried pease? He is born to be rich. He is thoroughly related; and is tempted out by his appetites and fancies to the conquest of this and that piece of nature, until he finds his well-being in the use of his planet, and of more planets than his own. Wealth requires, besides the crust of bread and the roof,—the freedom of the city, the freedom of the earth, traveling, machinery, the benefits of science, music, and fine arts, the best culture, and the best company. He is the rich man who can avail himself of all men's faculties. He is the richest man who knows how to draw a benefit from the labors of the greatest number of men, of men in distant countries, and in past times. The same correspondence that is between thirst in the stomach, and water in the spring, exists between the whole of man and the whole of nature. The elements offer their service to him. The sea, washing the equator and the poles, offers its perilous aid, and the power and empire that follow it,—day by day to his craft and audacity. "Beware of me," it says, "but if you can hold me, I am the key to all the lands." Fire offers, on its side, an equal power. Fire, steam, lightning, gravity, ledges of rock, mines of iron, lead, quicksilver, tin, and gold; forests of all woods; fruits of all climates; animals of all habits; the powers of tillage; the fabrics of his chemic laboratory; the webs of his loom; the masculine draught of his locomotive, the talismans of the machine-shop; all grand and subtle things, minerals, gases, ethers, passions, war, trade, government, are his natural playmates, and, according to the excellence of the machinery in each human being, is his attraction for the instruments he is to employ. The world is his tool-chest, and he is successful, or his education is carried on just so far, as is the marriage of his faculties with nature, or, the degree in which he takes up things into himself.

The strong race is strong on these terms. The Saxons are the merchants of the world; now, for a thousand years, the leading race, and by nothing more than their quality of personal independence, and, in its special modification, pecuniary independence. No reliance for bread and games on the government, no clanship, no patriarchal style of living by the revenues of a chief, no marrying-on,—no system of clientship suits them; but every man must pay his scot. The English are prosperous and peaceable, with their habit of considering that every man must take care of himself, and has himself to thank, if he do not maintain and improve his position in society.

The subject of economy mixes itself with morals, inasmuch as it is a peremptory point of virtue that a man's independence be secured. Poverty demoralizes. A man in debt is so far a slave; and Wall-street thinks it easy for a *millionaire* to be a man of his word, a man of honor, but, that, in failing circumstances, no man can be relied on to keep his integrity. And when one observes in the hotels and palaces of our Atlantic capitals, the habit of expense, the riot of the senses, the absence of bonds, clanship, fellow-feeling of any kind, he feels, that, when a man or a woman is driven to the wall, the chances of integrity are frightfully diminished, as if virtue were coming to be a luxury which few could afford, or, as Burke said, "at a market almost too high for humanity." He may fix his inventory of necessities and of enjoyments on what scale he pleases, but if he wishes the power and privilege of thought, the chalking out his own career, and having society on his own terms, he must bring his wants within his proper power to satisfy.

The manly part is to do with might and main what you can do. The world is full of fops who never did anything, and who have persuaded beauties and men of genius to wear their fop livery, and these will deliver the fop opinion, that it is not respectable to be seen earning a living; that it is much more respectable to spend without earning; and this doctrine of the snake will come also from the elect sons of light; for wise men are not wise at all hours, and will speak five times from their taste or their humor, to once from their reason. The brave workman, who might betray his feeling of it in his manners, if he do not succumb in his practice, must replace the grace or elegance forfeited, by the merit of the work done. No matter whether he make shoes, or statues, or laws. It is the privilege of any human work which is well done to invest the doer with a certain haughtiness. He can well afford not to conciliate, whose faithful work will answer for him. The mechanic at his bench carries a quiet heart and assured manners, and deals on even terms with men of any condition. The artist has made his picture so true, that it disconcerts criticism. The statue is so beautiful, that it contracts no stain from the market, but makes the market a silent gallery for itself. The case of the young lawyer was pitiful to disgust,—a paltry matter of buttons or tweezer-cases; but the determined youth saw in it an aperture to insert his dangerous wedges, made the insignificance of the thing forgotten, and gave fame by his sense and energy to the name and affairs of the Tittleton snuffbox factory.

Society in large towns is babyish, and wealth is made a toy. The life of pleasure is so ostentatious, that a shallow observer must believe that this is the agreed best use of wealth, and, whatever is pretended, it ends in cosseting. But, if this were the main use of surplus capital, it would bring us to barricades, burned towns, and tomahawks, presently. Men of sense esteem wealth to be the assimilation of nature to themselves, the converting of the sap and juices of the planet to the incarnation and nutriment of their design. Power is what they want,—not candy;—power to execute their design, power to give legs and feet, form and actuality to their thought, which, to a clear-sighted man, appears the end for which the Universe exists, and all its resources might be well applied. Columbus thinks that the sphere is a problem for practical navigation, as well as for closet geometry, and looks on all kings and peoples as cowardly landsmen, until they dare fit him out. Few men on the planet have more truly belonged to it. But he was forced to leave much of his map blank. His successors inherited his map, and inherited his fury to complete it.

So the men of the mine, telegraph, mill, map, and survey,—the monomaniacs, who talk up their project in marts, and offices, and entreat men to subscribe:—how did our factories get built? how did North America get netted with iron rails, except by the importunity of these orators, who dragged all the prudent men in? Is party the madness of many for the gain of a few? This speculative genius is the madness of few for the gain of the world. The projectors are sacrificed, but the public is the gainer. Each of these idealists, working after his thought, would make it tyrannical, if he could. He is met and antagonized by other speculators, as hot as he. The equilibrium is preserved by these counteractions, as one tree keeps down another in the forest, that it may not absorb all the sap in the ground. And the supply in nature of railroad presidents, copper-miners, grand-junctioners, smoke-burners, fire-annihilators, &c., is limited by the same law which keeps the proportion in the supply of carbon, of alum, and of hydrogen.

To be rich is to have a ticket of admission to the master-works and chief men of each race. It is to have the sea, by voyaging; to visit the mountains, Niagara, the Nile, the desert, Rome, Paris, Constantinople; to see galleries, libraries, arsenals, manufactories. The reader of Humboldt's "Cosmos" follows the marches of a man whose eyes, ears, and mind are armed by all the science, arts, and implements which mankind have anywhere accumulated, and who is using these to add to the stock. So is it with Denon, Beckford, Belzoni, Wilkinson, Layard, Kane, Lepsius, and Livingston. "The rich man," says Saadi, "is everywhere expected and at home." The rich take up something more of the world into man's life. They include the country as well as the town, the ocean-side, the White Hills, the Far West, and the old European homesteads of man, in their notion of available material. The world is his, who has money to go over it. He arrives at the sea-shore, and a sumptuous ship has floored and carpeted for him the stormy Atlantic, and made it a luxurious hotel, amid the horrors of tempests. The Persians say, "'Tis the same to him who wears a shoe, as if the whole earth were covered with leather."

Kings are said to have long arms, but every man should have long arms, and should pluck his living, his instruments, his power, and his knowing, from the sun, moon, and stars. Is not then the demand to be rich legitimate? Yet, I have never seen a rich man. I have never seen a man as rich as all men ought to be, or, with an adequate command of nature. The pulpit and the press have many commonplaces denouncing the thirst for wealth; but if men should take these moralists at their word, and leave off aiming to be rich, the moralists would rush to rekindle at all hazards this love of power in the people, lest civilization should be undone. Men are urged by their ideas to acquire the command over nature. Ages derive a culture from the wealth of Roman Caesars, Leo Tenths, magnificent Kings of France, Grand Dukes of Tuscany, Dukes of Devonshire, Townleys, Vernons, and Peels, in England; or whatever great proprietors. It is the interest of all men, that there should be Vaticans and Louvres full of noble works of art; British Museums, and French Gardens of Plants, Philadelphia Academies of Natural History, Bodleian, Ambrosian, Royal, Congressional Libraries. It is the interest of all that there should be Exploring Expeditions; Captain Cooks to voyage round the world, Rosses, Franklins, Richardsons, and Kanes, to find the magnetic and the geographic poles. We are all richer for the measurement of a degree of latitude on the earth's surface. Our navigation is safer for the chart. How intimately our knowledge of the system of the Universe rests on that!—and a true economy in a state or an individual will forget its frugality in behalf of claims like these.

Whilst it is each man's interest, that, not only ease and convenience of living, but also wealth or surplus product should exist somewhere, it need not be in his hands. Often it is very undesirable to him. Goethe said well, "nobody should be rich but those who understand it." Some men are born to own, and can animate all their possessions. Others cannot: their owning is not graceful; seems to be a compromise of their character: they seem to steal their own dividends. They should own who can administer; not they who hoard and conceal; not they who, the greater proprietors they are, are only the greater beggars, but they whose work carves out work for more, opens a path for all. For he is the rich man in whom the people are rich, and he is the poor man in whom the people are poor: and how to give all access to the masterpieces of art and nature, is the problem of civilization. The socialism of our day has done good service in setting men on thinking how certain civilizing benefits, now only enjoyed by the opulent, can be enjoyed by all. For example, the providing to each man the means and apparatus of science, and of the arts. There are many articles good for occasional use, which few men are able to own. Every man wishes to see the ring of Saturn, the satellites and belts of Jupiter and Mars; the mountains and craters in the moon: yet how few can buy a telescope! and of those, scarcely one would like the trouble of keeping it in order, and exhibiting it. So of electrical and chemical apparatus, and many the like things. Every man may have occasion to consult books which he does not care to possess, such as encyclopedias, dictionaries, tables, charts, maps, and public documents: pictures also of birds, beasts, fishes, shells, trees, flowers, whose names he desires to know.

There is a refining influence from the arts of Design on a prepared mind, which is as positive as that of music, and not to be supplied from any other source. But pictures, engravings, statues, and casts, beside their first cost, entail expenses, as of galleries and keepers for the exhibition; and the use which any man can make of them is rare, and their value, too, is much enhanced by the numbers of men who can share their enjoyment. In the Greek cities, it was reckoned profane, that any person should pretend a property in a work of art, which belonged to all who could behold it. I think sometimes,—could I only have music on my own terms;—could I live in a great city, and know where I could go whenever I wished the ablution and inundation of musical waves,—that were a bath and a medicine.

If properties of this kind were owned by states, towns, and lyceums, they would draw the bonds of neighborhood closer. A town would exist to an intellectual purpose. In Europe, where the feudal forms secure the permanence of wealth in certain families, those families buy and preserve these things, and lay them open to the public. But in America, where democratic institutions divide every estate into small portions, after a few years, the public should step into the place of these proprietors, and provide this culture and inspiration for the citizen.

Man was born to be rich, or, inevitably grows rich by the use of his faculties; by the union of thought with nature. Property is an intellectual production. The game requires coolness, right reasoning, promptness, and patience in the players. Cultivated labor drives out brute labor. An infinite number of shrewd men, in infinite years, have arrived at certain best and shortest ways of doing, and this accumulated skill in arts, cultures, harvestings, curings, manufactures, navigations, exchanges, constitutes the worth of our world today.

Commerce is a game of skill, which every man cannot play, which few men can play well. The right merchant is one who has the just average of faculties we call *common sense*; a man of a strong affinity for facts, who makes up his decision on what he has seen. He is thoroughly persuaded of the truths of arithmetic. There is always a reason, *in the man*, for his good or bad fortune, and so, in making money. Men talk as if there were some magic about this, and believe in magic, in all parts of life. He knows, that all goes on the old road, pound for pound, cent for cent,—for every effect a perfect cause,—and that good luck is another name for tenacity of purpose. He insures himself in every transaction, and likes small and sure gains. Probity and closeness to the facts are the basis, but the masters of the art add a certain long arithmetic. The problem is, to combine many and remote operations, with the accuracy and adherence to the facts, which is easy in near and small transactions; so to arrive at gigantic results, without any compromise of safety. Napoleon was fond of telling the story of the Marseilles banker, who said to his visitor, surprised at the contrast between the splendor of the banker's chateau and hospitality, and the meanness of the counting-room in which he had seen him,—"Young man, you are too young to understand how masses are formed,—the true and only power,—whether composed of money, water, or men, it is all alike,—a mass is an immense centre of motion, but it must be begun, it must be kept up:"—and he might have added, that the way in which it must be begun and kept up, is, by obedience to the law of particles.

Success consists in close appliance to the laws of the world, and, since those laws are intellectual and moral, an intellectual and moral obedience. Political Economy is as good a book wherein to read the life of man, and the ascendency of laws over all private and hostile influences, as any Bible which has come down to us.

Money is representative, and follows the nature and fortunes of the owner. The coin is a delicate meter of civil, social, and moral changes. The farmer is covetous of his dollar, and with reason. It is no waif to him. He knows how many strokes of labor it represents. His bones ache with the day's work that earned it. He knows how much land it represents;—how much rain, frost, and sunshine. He knows that, in the dollar, he gives you so much discretion and patience so much hoeing, and threshing. Try to lift his dollar; you must lift all that weight. In the city, where money follows the skit of a pen, or a lucky rise in exchange, it comes to be looked on as light. I wish the farmer held it dearer, and would spend it only for real bread; force for force.

The farmer's dollar is heavy, and the clerk's is light and nimble; leaps out of his pocket; jumps on to cards and faro-tables: but still more curious is its susceptibility to metaphysical changes. It is the finest barometer of social storms, and announces revolutions.

Every step of civil advancement makes every man's dollar worth more. In California, the country where it grew,—what would it buy? A few years since, it would buy a shanty, dysentery, hunger, bad company, and crime. There are wide countries, like Siberia, where it would buy little else today, than some petty mitigation of suffering. In Rome, it will buy beauty and magnificence. Forty years ago, a dollar would not buy much in Boston. Now it will buy a great deal more in our old town, thanks to railroads, telegraphs, steamers, and the contemporaneous growth of New York, and the whole country. Yet there are many goods appertaining to a capital city, which are not yet purchasable here, no, not with a mountain of dollars. A dollar in Florida is not worth a dollar in Massachusetts. A dollar is not value, but representative of value, and, at last, of moral values. A dollar is rated for the corn it will buy, or to speak strictly, not for the corn or house-room, but for Athenian corn, and Roman house-room,—for the wit, probity, and power, which we eat bread and dwell in houses to share and exert. Wealth is mental; wealth is moral. The value of a dollar is, to buy just things: a dollar goes on increasing in value with all the genius, and all the virtue of the world. A dollar in a university, is worth more than a dollar in a jail; in a temperate, schooled, law-abiding community, than in some sink of crime, where dice, knives, and arsenic, are in constant play.

The "Bank-Note Detector" is a useful publication. But the current dollar, silver or paper, is itself the detector of the right and wrong where it circulates. Is it not instantly enhanced by the increase of equity? If a trader refuses to sell his vote, or adheres to some odious right, he makes so much more equity in Massachusetts; and every acre in the State is more worth, in the hour of his action. If you take out of State-street the ten honestest merchants, and put in ten roguish persons, controlling the same amount of capital,—the rates of insurance will indicate it; the soundness of banks will show it: the highways will be less secure: the schools will feel it; the children will bring home their little dose of the poison: the judge will sit less firmly on the bench, and his decisions be less upright; he has lost so much support and constraint,—which all need; and the pulpit will betray it, in a laxer rule of life. An apple-tree, if you take out every day for a number of days, a load of loam, and put in a load of sand about its roots,—will find it out. An apple-tree is a stupid kind of creature, but if this treatment be pursued for a short time, I think it would begin to mistrust something. And if you should take out of the powerful class engaged in trade a hundred good men, and put in a hundred bad, or, what is just the same thing, introduce a demoralizing institution, would not the dollar, which is not much stupider than an apple-tree, presently find it out? The value of a dollar is social, as it is created by society. Every man who removes into this city, with any purchasable talent or skill in him, gives to every man's labor in the city, a new worth. If a talent is anywhere born into the world, the community of nations is enriched; and, much more, with a new degree of probity. The expense of crime, one of the principal charges of every nation, is so far stopped. In Europe, crime is observed to increase or abate with the price of bread. If the Rothschilds at Paris do not accept bills, the people at Manchester, at Paisley, at Birmingham, are forced into the highway, and landlords are shot down in Ireland. The police records attest it. The vibrations are presently felt in New York, New Orleans, and Chicago. Not much otherwise, the economical power touches the masses through the political lords. Rothschild refuses the Russian loan, and there is peace, and the harvests are saved. He takes it, and there is war, and an agitation through a large portion of mankind, with every hideous result, ending in revolution, and a new order.

Wealth brings with it its own checks and balances. The basis of political economy is non-interference. The only safe rule is found in the self-adjusting meter of demand and supply. Do not legislate. Meddle, and you snap the sinews with your sumptuary laws. Give no bounties: make equal laws: secure life and property, and you need not give alms. Open the doors of opportunity to talent and virtue, and they will do themselves justice, and property will not be in bad hands. In a free and just commonwealth, property rushes from the idle and imbecile, to the industrious, brave, and persevering.

The laws of nature play through trade, as a toy-battery exhibits the effects of electricity. The level of the sea is not more surely kept, than is the equilibrium of value in society, by the demand and supply: and artifice or legislation punishes itself, by reactions, gluts, and bankruptcies. The sublime laws play indifferently through atoms and galaxies. Whoever knows what happens in the getting and spending of a loaf of bread and a pint of beer; that no wishing will change the rigorous limits of pints and penny loaves; that, for all that is consumed, so much less remains in the basket and pot; but what is gone out of these is not wasted, but well spent, if it nourish his body, and enable him to finish his task;—knows all of political economy that the budgets of empires can teach him. The interest of petty economy is this symbolization of the great economy; the way in which a house, and a private man's methods, tally with the solar system, and the laws of give and take, throughout nature; and, however wary we are of the falsehoods and petty tricks which we suicidally play off on each other, every man has a certain satisfaction, whenever his dealing touches on the inevitable facts; when he sees that things themselves dictate the price, as they always tend to do, and, in large manufactures, are seen to do. Your paper is not fine or coarse enough,—is too heavy, or too thin. The manufacturer says, he will furnish you with just that thickness or thinness you want; the pattern is quite indifferent to him; here is his schedule;—any variety of paper, as cheaper or dearer, with the prices annexed. A pound of paper costs so much, and you may have it made up in any pattern you fancy.

There is in all our dealings a self-regulation that supersedes chaffering. You will rent a house, but must have it cheap. The owner can reduce the rent, but so he incapacitates himself from making proper repairs, and the tenant gets not the house he would have, but a worse one; besides, that a relation a little injurious is established between land-lord and tenant. You dismiss your laborer, saying, "Patrick, I shall send for you as soon as I cannot do without you." Patrick goes off contented, for he knows that the weeds will grow with the potatoes, the vines must be planted, next week, and, however unwilling you may be, the cantaloupes, crook-necks, and cucumbers will send for him. Who but must wish that all labor and value should stand on the same simple and surly market? If it is the best of its kind, it will. We must have joiner, locksmith, planter, priest, poet, doctor, cook, weaver, ostler; each in turn, through the year.

If a St. Michael's pear sells for a shilling, it costs a shilling to raise it. If, in Boston, the best securities offer twelve per cent. for money, they have just six per cent. of insecurity. You may not see that the fine pear costs you a shilling, but it costs the community so much. The shilling represents the number of enemies the pear has, and the amount of risk in ripening it. The price of coal shows the narrowness of the coal-field, and a compulsory confinement of the miners to a certain district. All salaries are reckoned on contingent, as well as on actual services. "If the wind were always southwest by west," said the skipper, "women might take ships to sea." One might say, that all things are of one price; that nothing is cheap or dear; and that the apparent disparities that strike us, are only a shopman's trick of concealing the damage in your bargain. A youth coming into the city from his native New Hampshire farm, with its hard fare still fresh in his remembrance, boards at a first-class hotel, and believes he must somehow have outwitted Dr. Franklin and Malthus, for luxuries are cheap. But he pays for the one convenience of a better dinner, by the loss of some of the richest social and educational advantages. He has lost what guards! what incentives! He will perhaps find by and by, that he left the Muses at the door of the hotel, and found the Furies inside. Money often costs too much, and power and pleasure are not cheap. The ancient poet said, "the gods sell all things at a fair price."

There is an example of the compensations in the commercial history of this country. When the European wars threw the carrying-trade of the world, from 1800 to 1812, into American bottoms, a seizure was now and then made of an American ship. Of course, the loss was serious to the owner, but the country was indemnified; for we charged threepence a pound for carrying cotton, sixpence for tobacco, and so on; which paid for the risk and loss, and brought into the country an immense prosperity, early marriages, private wealth, the building of cities, and of states: and, after the war was over, we received compensation over and above, by treaty, for all the seizures. Well, the Americans grew rich and great. But the pay-day comes round. Britain, France, and Germany, which our extraordinary profits had impoverished, send out, attracted by the fame of our advantages, first their thousands, then their millions, of poor people, to share the crop. At first, we employ them, and increase our prosperity: but, in the artificial system of society and of protected labor, which we also have adopted and enlarged, there come presently checks and stoppages. Then we refuse to employ these poor men. But they will not so be answered. They go into the poor rates, and, though we refuse wages, we must now pay the same amount in the form of taxes. Again, it turns out that the largest proportion of crimes are committed by foreigners. The cost of the crime, and the expense of courts, and of prisons, we must bear, and the standing army of preventive police we must pay. The cost of education of the posterity of this great colony, I will not compute. But the gross amount of these costs will begin to pay back what we thought was a net gain from our transatlantic customers of 1800. It is vain to refuse this payment. We cannot get rid of these people, and we cannot get rid of their will to be supported. That has become an inevitable element of our politics; and, for their votes, each of the dominant parties courts and assists them to get it executed. Moreover, we have to pay, not what would have contented them at home, but what they have learned to think necessary here; so that opinion, fancy, and all manner of moral considerations complicate the problem.

There are a few measures of economy which will bear to be named without disgust; for the subject is tender, and we may easily have too much of it; and therein resembles the hideous animalcules of which our bodies are built up,—which, offensive in the particular, yet compose valuable and effective masses. Our nature and genius force us to respect ends, whilst we use means. We must use the means, and yet, in our most accurate using, somehow screen and cloak them, as we can only give them any beauty, by a reflection of the glory of the end. That is the good head, which serves the end, and commands the means. The rabble are corrupted by their means: the means are too strong for them, and they desert their end.

I. The first of these measures is that each man's expense must proceed from his character. As long as your genius buys, the investment is safe, though you spend like a monarch. Nature arms each man with some faculty which enables him to do easily some feat impossible to any other, and thus makes him necessary to society. This native determination guides his labor and his spending. He wants an equipment of means and tools proper to his talent. And to save on this point, were to neutralize the special strength and helpfulness of each mind. Do your work, respecting the excellence of the work, and not its acceptableness. This is so much economy, that, rightly read, it is the sum of economy. Profligacy consists not in spending years of time or chests of money,—but in spending them off the line of your career. The crime which bankrupts men and states, is, jobwork;—declining from your main design, to serve a turn here or there. Nothing is beneath you, if it is in the direction of your life: nothing is great or desirable, if it is off from that. I think we are entitled here to draw a straight line, and say, that society can never prosper, but must always be bankrupt, until every man does that which he was created to do.

Spend for your expense, and retrench the expense which is not yours. Allston, the painter, was wont to say, that he built a plain house, and filled it with plain furniture, because he would hold out no bribe to any to visit him, who had not similar tastes to his own. We are sympathetic, and, like children, want everything we see. But it is a large stride to independence,— when a man, in the discovery of his proper talent, has sunk the necessity for false expenses. As the betrothed maiden, by one secure affection, is relieved from a system of slaveries,—the daily inculcated necessity of pleasing all,—so the man who has found what he can do, can spend on that, and leave all other spending. Montaigne said, "When he was a younger brother, he went brave in dress and equipage, but afterward his chateau and farms might answer for him." Let a man who belongs to the class of nobles, those, namely, who have found out that they can do something, relieve himself of all vague squandering on objects not his. Let the realist not mind appearances. Let him delegate to others the costly courtesies and decorations of social life. The virtues are economists, but some of the vices are also. Thus, next to humility, I have noticed that pride is a pretty good husband. A good pride is, as I reckon it, worth from five hundred to fifteen hundred a year. Pride is handsome, economical: pride eradicates so many vices, letting none subsist but itself, that it seems as if it were a great gain to exchange vanity for pride. Pride can go without domestics, without fine clothes, can live in a house with two rooms, can eat potato, purslain, beans, lyed corn, can work on the soil, can travel afoot, can talk with poor men, or sit silent well-contented in fine saloons. But vanity costs money, labor, horses, men, women, health, and peace, and is still nothing at last, a long way leading nowhere.—Only one drawback; proud people are intolerably selfish, and the vain are gentle and giving.

Art is a jealous mistress, and, if a man have a genius for painting, poetry, music, architecture, or philosophy, he makes a bad husband, and an ill provider, and should be wise in season, and not fetter himself with duties which will embitter his days, and spoil him for his proper work. We had in this region, twenty years ago, among our educated men, a sort of Arcadian fanaticism, a passionate desire to go upon the land, and unite farming to intellectual pursuits. [The Brook Farm—*ed.*] Many effected their purpose, and made the experiment, and some became downright ploughmen; but all were cured of their faith that scholarship and practical farming, (I mean, with one's own hands,) could be united.

With brow bent, with firm intent, the pale scholar leaves his desk to draw a freer breath, and get a juster statement of his thought, in the garden-walk. He stoops to pull up a purslain, or a dock, that is choking the young corn, and finds there are two: close behind the last, is a third; he reaches out his hand to a fourth; behind that, are four thousand and one. He is heated and untuned, and, by and by, wakes up from his idiot dream of chickweed and red-root, to remember his morning thought, and to find, that, with his adamantine purposes, he has been duped by a dandelion. A garden is like those pernicious machineries we read of, every month, in the newspapers, which catch a man's coat-skirt or his hand, and draw in his arm, his leg, and his whole body to irresistible destruction. In an evil hour he pulled down his wall, and added a field to his homestead. No land is bad, but land is worse. If a man own land, the land owns him. Now let him leave home, if he dare. Every tree and graft, every hill of melons, row of corn, or quickset hedge, all he has done, and all he means to do, stand in his way, like duns, when he would go out of his gate. The devotion to these vines and trees he finds poisonous. Long free walks, a circuit of miles, free his brain, and serve his body. Long marches are no hardship to him. He believes he composes easily on the hills. But this pottering in a few square yards of garden is dispiriting and driveling. The smell of the plants has drugged him, and robbed him of energy. He finds a catalepsy in his bones. He grows peevish and poor-spirited. The genius of reading and of gardening are antagonistic, like resinous and vitreous electricity. One is concentrative in sparks and shocks: the other is diffuse strength; so that each disqualifies its workman for the other's duties.

An engraver whose hands must be of an exquisite delicacy of stroke, should not lay stone walls. Sir David Brewster gives exact instructions for microscopic observation:—"Lie down on your back, and hold the single lens and object over your eye," &c. &c. How much more the seeker of abstract truth, who needs periods of isolation, and rapt concentration, and almost a going out of the body to think!

2. Spend after your genius, *and by system*. Nature goes by rule, not by sallies and saltations. There must be system in the economies. Saving and inexpensiveness will not keep the most pathetic family from ruin, nor will bigger incomes make free spending safe. The secret of success lies never in the amount of money, but in the relation of income to outgo; as if, after expense has been fixed at a certain point, then new and steady rills of income, though never so small, being added, wealth begins. But in ordinary, as means increase, spending increases faster, so that, large incomes, in England and elsewhere, are found not to help matters;—the eating quality of debt does not relax its voracity. When the cholera is in the potato, what is the use of planting larger crops? In England, the richest country in the universe, I was assured by shrewd observers, that great lords and ladies had no more guineas to give away than other people; that liberality with money

is as rare, and as immediately famous a virtue as it is here. Want is a growing giant whom the coat of Have was never large enough to cover. I remember in Warwickshire, to have been shown a fair manor, still in the same name as in Shakespeare's time. The rent-roll, I was told, is some fourteen thousand pounds a year: but, when the second son of the late proprietor was born, the father was perplexed how to provide for him. The eldest son must inherit the manor; what to do with this supernumerary? He was advised to breed him for the Church, and to settle him in the rectorship, which was in the gift of the family; which was done. It is a general rule in that country, that bigger incomes do not help anybody. It is commonly observed, that a sudden wealth, like a prize drawn in a lottery, or a large bequest to a poor family, does not permanently enrich. They have served no apprenticeship to wealth, and, with the rapid wealth, come rapid claims: which they do not know how to deny, and the treasure is quickly dissipated.

A system must be in every economy, or the best single expedients are of no avail. A farm is a good thing, when it begins and ends with itself, and does not need a salary, or a shop, to eke it out. Thus, the cattle are a main link in the chain-ring. If the non-conformist or aesthetic farmer leaves out the cattle, and does not also leave out the want which the cattle must supply, he must fill the gap by begging or stealing. When men now alive were born, the farm yielded everything that was consumed on it. The farm yielded no money, and the farmer got on without. If he fell sick, his neighbors came in to his aid: each gave a day's work; or a half day; or lent his yoke of oxen, or his horse, and kept his work even: hoed his potatoes, mowed his hay, reaped his rye; well knowing that no man could afford to hire labor, without selling his land. In autumn, a farmer could sell an ox or a hog, and get a little money to pay taxes withal. Now, the farmer buys almost all he consumes,—tin-ware, cloth, sugar, tea, coffee, fish, coal, railroad-tickets, and newspapers.

A master in each art is required, because the practice is never with still or dead subjects, but they change in your hands. You think farm-buildings and broad acres a solid property: but its value is flowing like water. It requires as much watching as if you were decanting wine from a cask. The farmer knows what to do with it, stops every leak, turns all the streamlets to one reservoir, and decants wine: but a blunderhead comes out of Cornhill, tries his hand, and it all leaks away. So is it with granite streets, or timber townships, as with fruit or flowers. Nor is any investment so permanent, that it can be allowed to remain without incessant watching, as the history of each attempt to lock up an inheritance through two generations for an unborn inheritor may show.

When Mr. Cockayne takes a cottage in the country, and will keep his cow, he thinks a cow is a creature that is fed on hay, and gives a pail of milk twice a day. But the cow that he buys gives milk for three months; then her bag dries up. What to do with a dry cow? who will buy her? Perhaps he bought also a yoke of oxen to do his work; but they get blown and lame. What to do with blown and lame oxen? The farmer fats his, after the spring-work is done, and kills them in the fall. But how can Cockayne, who has no pastures, and leaves his cottage daily in the cars, at business hours, be pothered with fatting and killing oxen? He plants trees; but there must be crops, to keep the trees in ploughed land. What shall be the crops? He will have nothing to do with trees, but will have grass. After a year or two, the grass must be turned up and ploughed: now what crops? Credulous Cockayne!

3. Help comes in the custom of the country, and the rule of *Impera parendo*. The rule is not to dictate, nor to insist on carrying out each of your schemes by ignorant willfulness, but to learn practically the secret spoken from all nature, that things themselves refuse to be mismanaged, and will show to the watchful their own law. Nobody need stir hand or foot. The custom of the country will do it all. I know not how to build or to plant; neither how to buy wood, nor what to do with the house-lot, the field, or the wood-lot, when bought. Never fear: it is all settled how it shall be, long beforehand, in the custom of the country, whether to sand, or whether to clay it, when to plough, and how to dress, whether to grass, or to corn; and you cannot help or hinder it. Nature has her own best mode of doing each thing, and she has somewhere told it plainly, if we will keep our eyes and ears open. If not, she will not be slow in undeceiving us, when we prefer

our own way to hers. How often we must remember the art of the surgeon, which, in replacing the broken bone, contents itself with releasing the parts from false position; they fly into place by the action of the muscles. On this art of nature all our arts rely.

Of the two eminent engineers in the recent construction of railways in England, Mr. Brunel went straight from terminus to terminus, through mountains, over streams, crossing highways, cutting ducal estates in two, and shooting through this man's cellar, and that man's attic window, and so arriving at his end, at great pleasure to geometers, but with cost to his company. Mr. Stephenson, on the contrary, believing that the river knows the way, followed his valley, as implicitly as our Western Railroad follows the Westfield River, and turned out to be the safest and cheapest engineer. We say the cows laid out Boston. Well, there are worse surveyors. Every pedestrian in our pastures has frequent occasion to thank the cows for cutting the best path through the thicket, and over the hills: and travelers and Indians know the value of a buffalo-trail, which is sure to be the easiest possible pass through the ridge.

When a citizen, fresh from Dock-square, or Milk-street, comes out and buys land in the country, his first thought is to a fine outlook from his windows: his library must command a western view: a sunset every day, bathing the shoulder of Blue Hills, Wachusett, and the peaks of Monadnoc and Uncanoonuc. What, thirty acres, and all this magnificence for fifteen hundred dollars! It would be cheap at fifty thousand. He proceeds at once, his eyes dim with tears of joy, to fix the spot for his corner-stone. But the man who is to level the ground, thinks it will take many hundred loads of gravel to fill the hollow to the road. The stone-mason who should build the well thinks he shall have to dig forty feet: the baker doubts he shall never like to drive up to the door: the practical neighbor cavils at the position of the barn; and the citizen comes to know that his predecessor the farmer built the house in the right spot for the sun and wind, the spring, and water-drainage, and the convenience to the pasture, the garden, the field, and the road. So Dock-square yields the point, and things have their own way. Use has made the farmer wise, and the foolish citizen learns to take his counsel. From step to step he comes at last to surrender at discretion. The farmer affects to take his orders; but the citizen says, You may ask me as often as you will, and in what ingenious forms, for an opinion concerning the mode of building my wall, or sinking my well, or laying out my acre, but the ball will rebound to you. These are matters on which I neither know, nor need to know anything. These are questions which you and not I shall answer.

Not less, within doors, a system settles itself paramount and tyrannical over master and mistress, servant and child, cousin and acquaintance. 'Tis in vain that genius or virtue or energy of character strive and cry against it. This is fate. And 'tis very well that the poor husband reads in a book of a new way of living, and resolves to adopt it at home: let him go home and try it, if he dare.

4. Another point of economy is to look for seed of the same kind as you sow: and not to hope to buy one kind with another kind. Friendship buys friendship; justice, justice; military merit, military success. Good husbandry finds wife, children, and household. The good merchant large gains, ships, stocks, and money. The good poet fame, and literary credit; but not either, the other. Yet there is commonly a confusion of expectations on these points. Hotspur lives for the moment; praises himself for it; and despises Furlong, that he does not. Hotspur, of course, is poor; and Furlong a good provider. The odd circumstance is, that Hotspur thinks it a superiority in himself, this improvidence, which ought to be rewarded with Furlong's lands.

I have not at all completed my design. But we must not leave the topic, without casting one glance into the interior recesses. It is a doctrine of philosophy, that man is a being of degrees; that there is nothing in the world, which is not repeated in his body; his body being a sort of miniature or summary of the world: then that there is nothing in his body, which is not repeated as in a celestial sphere in his mind: then, there is nothing in his brain, which is not repeated in a higher sphere, in his moral system.

5. Now these things are so in Nature. All things ascend, and the royal rule of economy is, that it should ascend also, or, whatever we do must always

have a higher aim. Thus it is a maxim, that money is another kind of blood. *Pecunia alter sanguis*: or, the estate of a man is only a larger kind of body, and admits of regimen analogous to his bodily circulations. So there is no maxim of the merchant, e. g., "Best use of money is to pay debts;" "Every business by itself;" "Best time is present time;" "The right investment is in tools of your trade;" or the like, which does not admit of an extended sense. The counting-room maxims liberally expounded are laws of the Universe. The merchant's economy is a coarse symbol of the soul's economy. It is, to spend for power, and not for pleasure. It is to invest income; that is to say, to take up particulars into generals; days into integral eras,—literary, emotive, practical, of its life, and still to ascend in its investment. The merchant has but one rule, *absorb and invest*: he is to be capitalist: the scraps and filings must be gathered back into the crucible; the gas and smoke must be burned, and earnings must not go to increase expense, but to capital again. Well, the man must be capitalist. Will he spend his income, or will he invest? His body and every organ is under the same law. His body is a jar, in which the liquor of life is stored. Will he spend for pleasure? The way to ruin is short and facile. Will he not spend, but hoard for power? It passes through the sacred fermentations, by that law of Nature whereby everything climbs to higher platforms, and bodily vigor becomes mental and moral vigor. The bread he eats is first strength and animal spirits: it becomes, in higher laboratories, imagery and thought; and in still higher results, courage and endurance. This is the right compound interest; this is capital doubled, quadrupled, centupled; man raised to his highest power.

The true thrift is always to spend on the higher plane; to invest and invest, with keener avarice, that he may spend in spiritual creation, and not in augmenting animal existence. Nor is the man enriched, in repeating the old experiments of animal sensation, nor unless through new powers and ascending pleasures, he knows himself by the actual experience of higher good, to be already on the way to the highest.

Emerson's Keys to Success

Wealth is in applications of mind to nature; and the art of getting rich consists in a better order, in timeliness, in being at the right spot.

The craft of the merchant is this bringing a thing from where it abounds, to where it is costly.

He is the richest man who knows how to draw a benefit from the labors of the greatest number of men, of men in distant countries, and in past times.

Poverty demoralizes. A man in debt is so far a slave.

I have never seen a man as rich as all men ought to be, or, with an adequate command of nature.

To be rich is to have a ticket of admission to the master-works and chief men of each race.

He is the rich man in whom the people are rich, and he is the poor man in whom the people are poor.

Man was born to be rich, or, inevitably grows rich by the use of his faculties; by the union of thought with nature.

Good luck is another name for tenacity of purpose.

Money is representative, and follows the nature and fortunes of the owner.

Wealth is mental; wealth is moral.

In a free and just commonwealth, property rushes from the idle and imbecile, to the industrious, brave, and persevering.

Money often costs too much, and power and pleasure are not cheap.

Nature arms each man with some faculty which enables him to do easily some feat impossible to any other, and thus makes him necessary to society.

Nothing is beneath you, if it is in the direction of your life: nothing is great or desirable, if it is off from that.

The secret of success lies never in the amount of money, but in the relation of income to outgo.

Want is a growing giant whom the coat of Have was never large enough to cover.

Nature has her own best mode of doing each thing, and she has somewhere told it plainly, if we will keep our eyes and ears open.

Look for seed of the same kind as you sow: and not to hope to buy one kind with another kind. Friendship buys friendship; justice, justice; military merit, military success.

The merchant has but one rule, absorb and invest.

Sincerity

(Excerpted from Chapter VI of *The Conduct of Life*)

Shallow men believe in luck, believe in circumstances: It was somebody's name, or he happened to be there at the time, or, it was so then, and another day it would have been otherwise. Strong men believe in cause and effect. The man was born to do it, and his father was born to be the father of him and of this deed, and, by looking narrowly, you shall see there was no luck in the matter, but it was all a problem in arithmetic, or an experiment in chemistry. The curve of the flight of the moth is preordained, and all things go by number, rule, and weight.

Skepticism is unbelief in cause and effect. A man does not see, that, as he eats, so he thinks: as he deals, so he is, and so he appears; he does not see, that his son is the son of his thoughts and of his actions; that fortunes are not exceptions but fruits; that relation and connection are not somewhere and sometimes, but everywhere and always; no miscellany, no exemption, no anomaly,—but method, and an even web; and what comes out, that was put in. As we are, so we do; and as we do, so is it done to us; we are the builders of our fortunes; cant and lying and the attempt to secure a good which does not belong to us, are, once for all, balked and vain. But, in the human mind, this tie of fate is made alive. The law is the basis of the human mind. In us, it is inspiration; out there in Nature, we see its fatal strength. We call it the moral sentiment.

We owe to the Hindu Scriptures a definition of Law, which compares well with any in our Western books. "Law it is, which is without name, or color, or hands, or feet; which is smallest of the least, and largest of the large; all, and knowing all things; which hears without ears, sees without eyes, moves without feet, and seizes without hands."

If any reader tax me with using vague and traditional phrases, let me suggest to him, by a few examples, what kind of a trust this is, and how real. Let me show him that the dice are loaded; that the colors are fast, because they are the native colors of the fleece; that the globe is a battery, because every atom is a magnet; and that the police and sincerity of the Universe are secured by God's delegating his divinity to every particle; that there is no room for hypocrisy, no margin for choice.

The countryman leaving his native village, for the first time, and going abroad, finds all his habits broken up. In a new nation and language, his sect, as Quaker, or Lutheran, is lost. What! it is not then necessary to the order and existence of society? He misses this, and the commanding eye of his neighborhood, which held him to decorum. This is the peril of New York, of New Orleans, of London, of Paris, to young men. But after a little experience, he makes the discovery that there are no large cities,— none large enough to hide in; that the censors of action are as numerous and as near in Paris, as in Littleton or Portland; that the gossip is as prompt and vengeful. There is no concealment, and, for each offense, a several vengeance; that, reaction, or *nothing for nothing*, or, *things are as broad as they are long*, is not a rule for Littleton or Portland, but for the Universe.

We cannot spare the coarsest muniment of virtue. We are disgusted by gossip; yet it is of importance to keep the angels in their proprieties. The smallest fly will draw blood, and gossip is a weapon impossible to exclude from the privatest, highest, selectest. Nature created a police of many ranks. God has delegated himself to a million deputies. From these low external penalties, the scale ascends. Next come the resentments, the fears, which injustice calls out; then, the false relations in which the offender is put to other men; and the reaction of his fault on himself, in the solitude and devastation of his mind.

You cannot hide any secret. If the artist succor his flagging spirits by opium or wine, his work will characterize itself as the effect of opium or wine. If you make a picture or a statue, it sets the beholder in that state of mind you had, when you made it. If you spend for show, on building, or gardening, or on pictures, or on equipages, it will so appear. We are all physiognomists and penetrators of character, and things themselves are detective. If you follow the suburban fashion in building a sumptuous-looking house for a little money, it will appear to all eyes as a cheap dear house. There is no privacy that cannot be penetrated. No secret can be kept in the civilized world. Society is a masked ball, where every one hides his real character, and reveals it by hiding. If a man wish to conceal anything he carries, those whom he meets know that he conceals somewhat, and usually know what he conceals. Is it otherwise if there be some belief or some purpose he would bury in his breast? 'Tis as hard to hide as fire. He is a strong man who can hold down his opinion. A man cannot utter two or three sentences, without disclosing to intelligent ears precisely where he stands in life and thought, namely, whether in the kingdom of the senses and the understanding, or, in that of ideas and imagination, in the realm of intuitions and duty. People seem not to see that their opinion of the world is also a confession of character. We can only see what we are, and if we misbehave we suspect others. The fame of Shakespeare or of Voltaire, of Thomas a Kempis, or of Bonaparte, characterizes those who give it. As gas-light is found to be the best nocturnal police, so the universe protects itself by pitiless publicity.

Each must be armed—not necessarily with musket and pike. Happy, if, seeing these, he can feel that he has better muskets and pikes in his energy and constancy. To every creature is his own weapon, however skillfully concealed from himself, a good while. His work is sword and shield. Let him accuse none, let him injure none. The way to mend the bad world, is to create the right world. Here is a low political economy plotting to cut the throat of foreign competition, and establish our own;—excluding others by force, or making war on them; or, by cunning tariffs, giving preference to worse wares of ours. But the real and lasting victories are those of peace, and not of war. The way to conquer the foreign artisan, is, not to kill him, but to beat his work. And the Crystal Palaces and World Fairs, with their committees and prizes on all kinds of industry, are the result of this feeling. The American workman who strikes ten blows with his hammer, whilst the foreign workman only strikes one, is as really vanquishing that foreigner, as if the blows were aimed at and told on his person. I look on that man as happy, who, when there is question of success, looks into his work for a reply, not into the market, not into opinion, not into patronage. In every variety of human employment, in the mechanical and in the fine arts, in navigation, in farming, in legislating, there are among the numbers who do their task perfunctorily, as we say, or just to pass, and as badly as they dare,—there are the working-men, on whom the burden of the business falls,—those who love work, and love to see it rightly done, who finish their task for its own sake; and the state and the world is happy, that has the most of such finishers. The world will always do justice at last to such finishers: it cannot otherwise. He who has acquired the ability, may wait securely the occasion of making it felt and appreciated, and know that it will not loiter. Men talk as if victory were something fortunate. Work is victory. Wherever work is done, victory is obtained. There is no chance, and no blanks. You want but one verdict: if you have your own, you are secure of the rest. And yet, if witnesses are wanted, witnesses are near. There was never a man born so wise or good, but one or more companions came into the world with him, who delight in his faculty, and report it. I cannot see without awe, that no man thinks alone, and no man acts alone, but the divine assessors who came up with him into life,—now under one disguise, now under another,—like a police in citizens' clothes, walk with him, step for step, through all the kingdom of time.

    This reaction, this sincerity is the property of all things. To make our word or act sublime, we must make it real. It is our system that counts, not the single word or unsupported action. Use what language you will, you can never say anything but what you are. What I am, and what I think, is conveyed to you, in spite of my efforts to hold it back. What I am has been secretly conveyed from me to another, whilst I was vainly making up my mind to tell him it. He has heard from me what I never spoke.

    As men get on in life, they acquire a love for sincerity, and somewhat less solicitude to be lulled or amused. In the progress of the character, there is an increasing faith in the moral sentiment, and a decreasing faith in propositions. Young people admire talents, and particular excellences. As we grow older, we value total powers and effects, as the spirit, or quality of the man. We have another sight, and a new standard; an insight which disregards what is done for the eye, and pierces to the doer; an ear which hears not what men say, but hears what they do not say.

Emerson's Keys to Success

As we are, so we do; and as we do, so it is done to us; we are the builders of our fortunes.

No secret can be kept in the civilized world. Society is a masked ball, where every one hides his real character, and reveals it by hiding.

I look on that man as happy, who, when there is question of success, looks into his work for a reply.

Wherever work is done, victory is obtained.

Compensation

Man's the elm; Wealth the vine.

Ever since I was a boy, I have wished to write a discourse on Compensation: for it seemed to me when very young, that on this subject life was ahead of theology, and the people knew more than the preachers taught. The documents, too, from which the doctrine is to be drawn, charmed my fancy by their endless variety, and lay always before me, even in sleep; for they are the tools in our hands, the bread in our basket, the transactions of the street, the farm, and the dwelling-house, greetings, relations, debts and credits, the influence of character, the nature and endowment of all men. It seemed to me, also, that in it might be shown men a ray of divinity, the present action of the soul of this world, clean from all vestige of tradition, and so the heart of man might be bathed by an inundation of eternal love, conversing with that which he knows was always and always must be, because it really is now. It appeared, moreover, that if this doctrine could be stated in terms with any resemblance to those bright intuitions in which this truth is sometimes revealed to us, it would be a star in many dark hours and crooked passages in our journey that would not suffer us to lose our way.

I was lately confirmed in these desires by hearing a sermon at church. The preacher, a man esteemed for his orthodoxy, unfolded in the ordinary manner the doctrine of the Last Judgment. He assumed, that judgment is not executed in this world; that the wicked are successful; that the good are miserable; and then urged from reason and from Scripture a compensation to be made to both parties in the next life. No offense appeared to be taken by the congregation at this doctrine. As far as I could observe, when the meeting broke up, they separated without remark on the sermon.

Yet what was the import of this teaching? What did the preacher mean by saying that the good are miserable in the present life? Was it that houses and lands, offices, wine, horses, dress, luxury, are had by unprincipled men, whilst the saints are poor and despised; and that a compensation is to be made to these last hereafter, by giving them the like gratifications another day,—bank-stock and doubloons, venison and champagne? This must be the compensation intended; for what else? Is it that they are to have leave to pray and praise? to love and serve men? Why, that they can do now. The legitimate inference the disciple would draw was,—'We are to have *such* a good time as the sinners have now';—or, to push it to its extreme import,—'You sin now; we shall sin by and by; we would sin now, if we could; not being successful, we expect our revenge tomorrow.'

The fallacy lay in the immense concession, that the bad are successful; that justice is not done now. The blindness of the preacher consisted in deferring to the base estimate of the market of what constitutes a manly success, instead of confronting and convicting the world from the truth; announcing the presence of the soul; the omnipotence of the will: and so establishing the standard of good and ill, of success and falsehood.

I find a similar base tone in the popular religious works of the day, and the same doctrines assumed by the literary men when occasionally they treat the related topics. I think that our popular theology has gained in decorum, and not in principle, over the superstitions it has displaced. But men are better than this theology. Their daily life gives it the lie. Every ingenuous and aspiring soul leaves the doctrine behind him in his own experience; and all men feel sometimes the falsehood which they cannot demonstrate. For men are wiser than they know. That which they hear in schools and pulpits without after-thought, if said in conversation, would probably be questioned in silence. If a man dogmatize in a mixed company on Providence and the divine laws, he is answered by a silence which conveys well enough to an observer the dissatisfaction of the hearer, but his incapacity to make his own statement.

I shall attempt in this and the following chapter to record some facts that indicate the path of the law of Compensation; happy beyond my expectation, if I shall truly draw the smallest arc of this circle.

Polarity, or action and reaction, we meet in every part of nature; in darkness and light; in heat and cold; in the ebb and flow of waters; in male and female; in the inspiration and expiration of plants and animals; in the equation of quantity and quality in the fluids of the animal body; in the systole and diastole of the heart; in the undulations of fluids, and of sound; in the centrifugal and centripetal gravity; in electricity, galvanism, and chemical affinity. Superinduce magnetism at one end of a needle; the opposite magnetism takes place at the other end. If the south attracts, the north repels. To empty here, you must condense there. An inevitable dualism bisects nature, so that each thing is a half, and suggests another thing to make it whole; as, spirit, matter; man, woman; odd, even; subjective, objective; in, out; upper, under; motion, rest; yea, nay.

Whilst the world is thus dual, so is every one of its parts. The entire system of things gets represented in every particle. There is somewhat that resembles the ebb and flow of the sea, day and night, man and woman, in a single needle of the pine, in a kernel of corn, in each individual of every animal tribe. The reaction, so grand in the elements, is repeated within these small boundaries. For example, in the animal kingdom the physiologist has observed that no creatures are favorites, but a certain compensation balances every gift and every defect. A surplus given to one part is paid out of a reduction from another part of the same creature. If the head and neck are enlarged, the trunk and extremities are cut short.

The theory of the mechanic forces is another example. What we gain in power is lost in time; and the converse. The periodic or compensating errors of the planets is another instance. The influences of climate and soil in political history are another. The cold climate invigorates. The barren soil does not breed fevers, crocodiles, tigers, or scorpions.

The same dualism underlies the nature and condition of man. Every excess causes a defect; every defect an excess. Every sweet hath its sour; every evil its good. Every faculty which is a receiver of pleasure has an equal penalty put on its abuse. It is to answer for its moderation with its life. For every grain of wit there is a grain of folly. For every thing you have missed, you have gained something else; and for every thing you gain, you lose something. If riches increase, they are increased that use them. If the gatherer gathers too much, nature takes out of the man what she puts into his chest; swells the estate, but kills the owner. Nature hates monopolies and exceptions. The waves of the sea do not more speedily seek a level from their loftiest tossing, than the varieties of condition tend to equalize themselves. There is always some leveling circumstance that puts down the overbearing, the strong, the rich, the fortunate, substantially on the same ground with all others. Is a man too strong and fierce for society, and by temper and position a bad citizen,—a morose ruffian, with a dash of the pirate in him;—nature sends him a troop of pretty sons and daughters, who are getting along in the dame's classes at the village school, and love and fear for them smooths his grim scowl to courtesy. Thus she contrives to intenerate the granite and felspar, takes the boar out and puts the lamb in, and keeps her balance true.

The farmer imagines power and place are fine things. But the President has paid dear for his White House. It has commonly cost him all his peace, and the best of his manly attributes. To preserve for a short time so conspicuous an appearance before the world, he is content to eat dust before the real masters who stand erect behind the throne. Or, do men desire the more substantial and permanent grandeur of genius? Neither has this an immunity. He who by force of will or of thought is great, and overlooks thousands, has the charges of that eminence. With every influx of light comes new danger. Has he light? he must bear witness to the light, and always outrun that sympathy which gives him such keen satisfaction, by his fidelity to new revelations of the incessant soul. He must hate father and mother, wife and child. Has he all that the world loves and admires and covets?—he must cast behind him their admiration, and afflict them by faithfulness to his truth, and become a byword and a hissing.

This law writes the laws of cities and nations. It is in vain to build or plot or combine against it. Things refuse to be mismanaged long. *Res nolunt diu male administrari.* Though no checks to a new evil appear, the checks exist, and will appear. If the government is cruel, the governor's life is not safe. If you tax too high, the revenue will yield nothing. If you make the criminal code sanguinary, juries will not convict. If the law is too mild, private vengeance comes in. If the government is a terrific democracy, the pressure is resisted by an overcharge of energy in the citizen, and life glows with a fiercer flame. The true life and satisfactions of man seem to elude the utmost rigors or felicities of condition, and to establish themselves with great indifferency under all varieties of circumstances. Under all governments the influence of character remains the same,—in Turkey and in New England about alike. Under the primeval despots of Egypt, history honestly confesses that man must have been as free as culture could make him.

These appearances indicate the fact that the universe is represented in every one of its particles. Everything in nature contains all the powers of nature. Everything is made of one hidden stuff; as the naturalist sees one type under every metamorphosis, and regards a horse as a running man, a fish as a swimming man, a bird as a flying man, a tree as a rooted man. Each new form repeats not only the main character of the type, but part for part all the details, all the aims, furtherances, hindrances, energies, and whole system of every other. Every occupation, trade, art, transaction, is a compend of the world, and a correlative of every other. Each one is an entire emblem of human life; of its good and ill, its trials, its enemies, its course and its end. And each one must somehow accommodate the whole man, and recite all his destiny.

The world globes itself in a drop of dew. The microscope cannot find the animalcule which is less perfect for being little. Eyes, ears, taste, smell, motion, resistance, appetite, and organs of reproduction that take hold on eternity,—all find room to consist in the small creature. So do we put our life into every act. The true doctrine of omnipresence is, that God reappears with all his parts in every moss and cobweb. The value of the universe contrives to throw itself into every point. If the good is there, so is the evil; if the affinity, so the repulsion; if the force, so the limitation.

Thus is the universe alive. All things are moral. That soul, which within us is a sentiment, outside of us is a law. We feel its inspiration; out there in history we can see its fatal strength. "It is in the world, and the world was made by it." Justice is not postponed. A perfect equity adjusts its balance in all parts of life. *Oi chusoi Dios aei enpiptousi,*—The dice of God are always loaded. The world looks like a multiplication-table, or a mathematical equation, which, turn it how you will, balances itself. Take what figure you will, its exact value, nor more nor less, still returns to you. Every secret is told, every crime is punished, every virtue rewarded, every wrong redressed, in silence and certainty. What we call retribution is the universal necessity by which the whole appears wherever a part appears. If you see smoke, there must be fire. If you see a hand or a limb, you know that the trunk to which it belongs is there behind.

Every act rewards itself, or, in other words, integrates itself, in a twofold manner; first, in the thing, or in real nature; and secondly, in the circumstance, or in apparent nature. Men call the circumstance the retribution. The causal retribution is in the thing, and is seen by the soul. The retribution in the circumstance is seen by the understanding; it is inseparable from the thing, but is often spread over a long time, and so does not become distinct until after many years. The specific stripes may follow late after the offense, but they follow because they accompany it. Crime and punishment grow out of one stem. Punishment is a fruit that unsuspected ripens within the flower of the pleasure which concealed it. Cause and effect, means and ends, seed and fruit, cannot be severed; for the effect already blooms in the cause, the end preexists in the means, the fruit in the seed.

Whilst thus the world will be whole, and refuses to be disparted, we seek to act partially, to sunder, to appropriate; for example,—to gratify the senses, we sever the pleasure of the senses from the needs of the character. The ingenuity of man has always been dedicated to the solution of one problem,—how to detach the sensual sweet, the sensual strong, the sensual bright, &c., from the moral sweet, the moral deep, the moral fair; that is, again, to contrive to cut clean off this upper surface so thin as to leave it bottomless; to get a *one end*, without an *other end*. The soul says, Eat; the body would feast. The soul says, The man and woman shall be one flesh and one soul; the body would join the flesh only. The soul says, Have dominion over all things to the ends of virtue; the body would have the power over things to its own ends.

The soul strives amain to live and work through all things. It would be the only fact. All things shall be added unto it power, pleasure, knowledge, beauty. The particular man aims to be somebody; to set up for himself; to truck and higgle for a private good; and, in particulars, to ride, that he may ride; to dress, that he may be dressed; to eat, that he may eat; and to govern, that he may be seen. Men seek to be great; they would have offices, wealth, power, and fame. They think that to be great is to possess one side of nature,—the sweet, without the other side,—the bitter.

This dividing and detaching is steadily counteracted. Up to this day, it must be owned, no projector has had the smallest success. The parted water reunites behind our hand. Pleasure is taken out of pleasant things, profit out of profitable things, power out of strong things, as soon as we seek to separate them from the whole. We can no more halve things and get the sensual good, by itself, than we can get an inside that shall have no outside, or a light without a shadow. "Drive out nature with a fork, she comes running back."

Life invests itself with inevitable conditions, which the unwise seek to dodge, which one and another brags that he does not know; that they do not touch him;—but the brag is on his lips, the conditions are in his soul. If he escapes them in one part, they attack him in another more vital part. If he has escaped them in form, and in the appearance, it is because he has resisted his life, and fled from himself, and the retribution is so much death. So signal is the failure of all attempts to make this separation of the good from the tax, that the experiment would not be tried,—since to try it is to be mad,—but for the circumstance, that when the disease began in the will, of rebellion and separation, the intellect is at once infected, so that the man ceases to see God whole in each object, but is able to see the sensual allurement of an object, and not see the sensual hurt; he sees the mermaid's head, but not the dragon's tail; and thinks he can cut off that which he would have, from that which he would not have. "How secret art thou who dwellest in the highest heavens in silence, O thou only great

God, sprinkling with an unwearied Providence certain penal blindnesses upon such as have unbridled desires!"

The human soul is true to these facts in the painting of fable, of history, of law, of proverbs, of conversation. It finds a tongue in literature unawares. Thus the Greeks called Jupiter, Supreme Mind; but having traditionally ascribed to him many base actions, they involuntarily made amends to reason, by tying up the hands of so bad a god. He is made as helpless as a king of England. Prometheus knows one secret which Jove must bargain for; Minerva, another. He cannot get his own thunders; Minerva keeps the key of them.

> "Of all the gods, I only know the keys
> That open the solid doors within whose vaults
> His thunders sleep."

A plain confession of the in-working of the All, and of its moral aim. The Indian mythology ends in the same ethics; and it would seem impossible for any fable to be invented and get any currency which was not moral. Aurora forgot to ask youth for her lover, and though Tithonus is immortal, he is old. Achilles is not quite invulnerable; the sacred waters did not wash the heel by which Thetis held him. Siegfried, in the Nibelungen, is not quite immortal, for a leaf fell on his back whilst he was bathing in the dragon's blood, and that spot which it covered is mortal. And so it must be. There is a crack in every thing God has made. It would seem, there is always this vindictive circumstance stealing in at unawares, even into the wild poesy in which the human fancy attempted to make bold holiday, and to shake itself free of the old laws,—this back-stroke, this kick of the gun, certifying that the law is fatal; that in nature nothing can be given, all things are sold.

This is that ancient doctrine of Nemesis, who keeps watch in the universe, and lets no offense go unchastised. The Furies, they said, are attendants on justice, and if the sun in heaven should transgress his path, they would punish him. The poets related that stone walls, and iron swords, and leathern thongs had an occult sympathy with the wrongs of their owners; that the belt which Ajax gave Hector dragged the Trojan hero over the field at the wheels of the car of Achilles, and the sword which Hector gave Ajax was that on whose point Ajax fell. They recorded, that when the Thasians erected a statue to Theagenes, a victor in the games, one of his rivals went to it by night, and endeavored to throw it down by repeated blows, until at last he moved it from its pedestal, and was crushed to death beneath its fall.

This voice of fable has in it somewhat divine. It came from thought above the will of the writer. That is the best part of each writer, which has nothing private in it; that which he does not know; that which flowed out of his constitution, and not from his too active invention; that which in the study of a single artist you might not easily find, but in the study of many, you would abstract as the spirit of them all. Phidias it is not, but the work of man in that early Hellenic world, that I would know. The name and circumstance of Phidias, however convenient for history, embarrass when we come to the highest criticism. We are to see that which man was tending to do in a given period, and was hindered, or, if you will, modified in doing, by the interfering volitions of Phidias, of Dante, of Shakespeare, the organ whereby man at the moment wrought.

Still more striking is the expression of this fact in the proverbs of all nations, which are always the literature of reason, or the statements of an absolute truth, without qualification. Proverbs, like the sacred books of each nation, are the sanctuary of the intuitions. That which the droning world, chained to appearances, will not allow the realist to say in his own words, it will suffer him to say in proverbs without contradiction. And this law of laws which the pulpit, the senate, and the college deny, is hourly preached in all markets and workshops by flights of proverbs, whose teaching is as true and as omnipresent as that of birds and flies.

All things are double, one against another.—Tit for tat; an eye for an eye; a tooth for a tooth; blood for blood; measure for measure; love for love.—Give and it shall be given you.—He that watereth shall be watered himself.—What will you have? quoth God; pay for it and take it.—Nothing venture, nothing have.—Thou shalt be paid exactly for what thou hast done, no more, no less.—Who doth not work shall not eat.—Harm watch, harm catch.—Curses always recoil on the head of him who imprecates them.—If you put a chain around the neck of a slave, the other end fastens itself around your own.—Bad counsel confounds the adviser.—The Devil is an ass.

It is thus written, because it is thus in life. Our action is overmastered and characterized above our will by the law of nature. We aim at a petty end quite aside from the public good, but our act arranges itself by irresistible magnetism in a line with the poles of the world.

A man cannot speak but he judges himself. With his will, or against his will, he draws his portrait to the eye of his companions by every word. Every opinion reacts on him who utters it. It is a thread-ball thrown at a mark, but the other end remains in the thrower's bag. Or, rather, it is a harpoon hurled at the whale, unwinding, as it flies, a coil of cord in the boat, and if the harpoon is not good, or not well thrown, it will go nigh to cut the steersman in twain, or to sink the boat.

You cannot do wrong without suffering wrong. "No man had ever a point of pride that was not injurious to him," said Burke. The exclusive in fashionable life does not see that he excludes himself from enjoyment, in the attempt to appropriate it. The exclusionist in religion does not see that he shuts the door of heaven on himself, in striving to shut out others. Treat men as pawns and ninepins, and you shall suffer as well as they. If you leave out their heart, you shall lose your own. The senses would make things of all persons; of women, of children, of the poor. The vulgar proverb, "I will get it from his purse or get it from his skin," is sound philosophy.

All infractions of love and equity in our social relations are speedily punished. They are punished by fear. Whilst I stand in simple relations to my fellow-man, I have no displeasure in meeting him. We meet as water meets water, or as two currents of air mix, with perfect diffusion and interpenetration of nature. But as soon as there is any departure from simplicity, and attempt at halfness, or good for me that is not good for him, my neighbor feels the wrong; he shrinks from me as far as I have shrunk from him; his eyes no longer seek mine; there is war between us; there is hate in him and fear in me.

All the old abuses in society, universal and particular, all unjust accumulations of property and power, are avenged in the same manner. Fear is an instructor of great sagacity, and the herald of all revolutions. One thing he teaches, that there is rottenness where he appears. He is a carrion crow, and though you see not well what he hovers for, there is death somewhere. Our property is timid, our laws are timid, our cultivated classes are timid. Fear for ages has boded and mowed and gibbered over government and property. That obscene bird is not there for nothing. He indicates great wrongs which must be revised.

Of the like nature is that expectation of change which instantly follows the suspension of our voluntary activity. The terror of cloudless noon, the emerald of Polycrates, the awe of prosperity, the instinct which leads every generous soul to impose on itself tasks of a noble asceticism and vicarious virtue, are the tremblings of the balance of justice through the heart and mind of man.

Experienced men of the world know very well that it is best to pay scot and lot as they go along, and that a man often pays dear for a small frugality. The borrower runs in his own debt. Has a man gained any thing who has received a hundred favors and rendered none? Has he gained by borrowing, through indolence or cunning, his neighbor's wares, or horses, or money? There arises on the deed the instant acknowledgment of benefit on the one part, and of debt on the other; that is, of superiority and inferiority. The transaction remains in the memory of himself and his neighbor; and every new transaction alters, according to its nature, their relation to each other. He may soon come to see that he had better have broken his own bones than to have ridden in his neighbors' coach, and that "the highest price he can pay for a thing is to ask for it."

A wise man will extend this lesson to all parts of life, and know that it is the part of prudence to face every claimant, and pay every just demand on your time, your talents, or your heart. Always pay; for, first or last, you must pay your entire debt. Persons and events may stand for a time between you and justice, but it is only a postponement. You must pay at last your own debt. If you are wise, you will dread a prosperity which only loads you with more. Benefit is the end of nature. But for every benefit which you receive, a tax is levied. He is great who confers the most benefits. He is base—and that is the one base thing in the universe—to receive favors and render none. In the order of nature we cannot render benefits to those from whom we receive them, or only seldom. But the benefit we receive must be rendered again, line for line, deed for deed, cent for cent, to somebody. Beware of too much good staying in your hand. It will fast corrupt and worm worms. Pay it away quickly in some sort.

Labor is watched over by the same pitiless laws. Cheapest, say the prudent, is the dearest labor. What we buy in a broom, a mat, a wagon, a knife, is some application of good sense to a common want. It is best to pay in your land a skillful gardener, or to buy good sense applied to gardening; in your sailor, good sense applied to navigation; in the house, good sense applied to cooking, sewing, serving; in your agent, good sense applied to accounts and affairs. So do you multiply your presence, or spread yourself throughout your estate. But because of the dual constitution of things, in labor as in life there can be no cheating. The thief steals from himself. The swindler swindles himself. For the real price of labor is knowledge and virtue, whereof wealth and credit are signs. These signs, like paper money, may be counterfeited or stolen, but that which they represent, namely, knowledge and virtue, cannot be counterfeited or stolen. These ends of labor cannot be answered but by real exertions of the mind, and in obedience to pure motives. The cheat, the defaulter, the gambler, cannot extort the knowledge of material and moral nature which his honest care and pains yield to the operative. The law of nature is, Do the thing, and you shall have the power: but they who do not the thing have not the power.

Human labor, through all its forms, from the sharpening of a stake to the construction of a city or an epic, is one immense illustration of the perfect compensation of the universe. The absolute balance of Give and Take, the doctrine that every thing has its price,—and if that price is not paid, not that thing but something else is obtained, and that it is impossible to get any thing without its price,—is not less sublime in the columns of a ledger than in the budgets of states, in the laws of light and darkness, in all the action and reaction of nature. I cannot doubt that the high laws which each man sees implicated in those processes with which he is conversant, the stern ethics which sparkle on his chisel-edge, which are measured out by his plumb and foot-rule, which stand as manifest in the footing of the shop-bill as in the history of a state,—do recommend to him his trade, and though seldom named, exalt his business to his imagination.

The league between virtue and nature engages all things to assume a hostile front to vice. The beautiful laws and substances of the world persecute and whip the traitor. He finds that things are arranged for truth and benefit, but there is no den in the wide world to hide a rogue. Commit a crime, and the earth is made of glass. Commit a crime, and it seems as if a coat of snow fell on the ground, such as reveals in the woods the track of every partridge and fox and squirrel and mole. You cannot recall the spoken word, you cannot wipe out the foot-track, you cannot draw up the ladder, so as to leave no inlet or clew. Some damning circumstance always transpires. The laws and substances of nature—water, snow, wind, gravitation—become penalties to the thief.

On the other hand, the law holds with equal sureness for all right action. Love, and you shall be loved. All love is mathematically just, as much as the two sides of an algebraic equation. The good man has absolute good, which like fire turns every thing to its own nature, so that you cannot do him any harm; but as the royal armies sent against Napoleon, when he approached, cast down their colors and from enemies became friends, so disasters of all kinds, as sickness, offense, poverty, prove benefactors:—

> "Winds blow and waters roll
> Strength to the brave, and power and deity,
> Yet in themselves are nothing."

The good are befriended even by weakness and defect. As no man had ever a point of pride that was not injurious to him, so no man had ever a defect that was not somewhere made useful to him. The stag in the fable admired his horns and blamed his feet, but when the hunter came, his feet saved him, and afterwards, caught in the thicket, his horns destroyed him. Every man in his lifetime needs to thank his faults. As no man thoroughly understands a truth until he has contended against it, so no man has a thorough acquaintance with the hindrances or talents of men, until he has suffered from the one, and seen the triumph of the other over his own want of the same. Has he a defect of temper that unfits him to live in society? Thereby he is driven to entertain himself alone, and acquire habits of self-help; and thus, like the wounded oyster, he mends his shell with pearl.

Our strength grows out of our weakness. The indignation which arms itself with secret forces does not awaken until we are pricked and stung and sorely assailed. A great man is always willing to be little. Whilst he sits on the cushion of advantages, he goes to sleep. When he is pushed, tormented, defeated, he has a chance to learn something; he has been put on his wits, on his manhood; he has gained facts; learns his ignorance; is cured of the insanity of conceit; has got moderation and real skill. The wise man throws himself on the side of his assailants. It is more his interest than it is theirs to find his weak point. The wound cicatrizes and falls off from him like a dead skin, and when they would triumph, lo! he has passed on invulnerable. Blame is safer than praise. I hate to be defended in a newspaper. As long as all that is said is said against me, I feel a certain assurance of success. But as soon as honeyed words of praise are spoken for me, I feel as one that lies unprotected before his enemies. In general, every evil to which we do not succumb is a benefactor. As the Sandwich Islander believes that the strength and valor of the enemy he kills passes into himself, so we gain the strength of the temptation we resist.

The same guards which protect us from disaster, defect, and enmity, defend us, if we will, from selfishness and fraud. Bolts and bars are not the best of our institutions, nor is shrewdness in trade a mark of wisdom. Men suffer all their life long, under the foolish superstition that they can be cheated. But it is as impossible for a man to be cheated by any one but himself, as for a thing to be and not to be at the same time. There is a third silent party to all our bargains. The nature and soul of things takes on itself the guaranty of the fulfillment of every contract, so that honest service cannot come to loss. If you serve an ungrateful master, serve him the more. Put God in your debt. Every stroke shall be repaid. The longer the payment is withholden, the better for you; for compound interest on compound interest is the rate and usage of this exchequer.

The history of persecution is a history of endeavors to cheat nature, to make water run up hill, to twist a rope of sand. It makes no difference whether the actors be many or one, a tyrant or a mob. A mob is a society of bodies voluntarily bereaving themselves of reason, and traversing its work. The mob is man voluntarily descending to the nature of the beast. Its fit hour of activity is night. Its actions are insane like its whole constitution. It persecutes a principle; it would whip a right; it would tar and feather justice, by inflicting fire and outrage upon the houses and persons of those who have these. It resembles the prank of boys, who run with fire-engines to put out the ruddy aurora streaming to the stars. The inviolate spirit turns their spite against the wrongdoers. The martyr cannot be dishonored. Every lash inflicted is a tongue of fame; every prison, a more illustrious abode; every burned book or house enlightens the world; every suppressed or expunged word reverberates through the earth from side to side. Hours of sanity and consideration are always arriving to communities, as to individuals, when the truth is seen, and the martyrs are justified.

Thus do all things preach the indifferency of circumstances. The man is all. Every thing has two sides, a good and an evil. Every advantage has its tax. I learn to be content. But the doctrine of compensation is not the doctrine of indifferency. The thoughtless say, on hearing these representations,—What boots it to do well? there is one event to good and evil; if I gain any good, I must pay for it; if I lose any good, I gain some other; all actions are indifferent.

There is a deeper fact in the soul than compensation, to wit, its own nature. The soul is not a compensation, but a life. The soul *is*. Under all this running sea of circumstance, whose waters ebb and flow with perfect balance, lies the aboriginal abyss of real Being. Essence, or God, is not a relation, or a part, but the whole. Being is the vast affirmative, excluding negation, self-balanced, and swallowing up all relations, parts, and times within itself. Nature, truth, virtue, are the influx from thence. Vice is the absence or departure of the same. Nothing, Falsehood, may indeed stand as the great Night or shade, on which, as a background, the living universe paints itself forth; but no fact is begotten by it; it cannot work; for it is not. It cannot work any good; it cannot work any harm. It is harm inasmuch as it is worse not to be than to be.

We feel defrauded of the retribution due to evil acts, because the criminal adheres to his vice and contumacy, and does not come to a crisis or judgment anywhere in visible nature. There is no stunning confutation of his nonsense before men and angels. Has he therefore outwitted the law? Inasmuch as he carries the malignity and the lie with him, he so far deceases from nature. In some manner there will be a demonstration of the wrong to the understanding also; but should we not see it, this deadly deduction makes square the eternal account.

Neither can it be said, on the other hand, that the gain of rectitude must be bought by any loss. There is no penalty to virtue; no penalty to wisdom; they are proper additions of being. In a virtuous action, I properly *am*; in a virtuous act, I add to the world; I plant into deserts conquered from Chaos and Nothing, and see the darkness receding on the limits of the horizon. There can be no excess to love; none to knowledge; none to beauty, when these attributes are considered in the purest sense. The soul refuses limits, and always affirms an Optimism, never a Pessimism.

His life is a progress, and not a station. His instinct is trust. Our instinct uses "more" and "less" in application to man, of the *presence of the soul*, and not of its absence; the brave man is greater than the coward; the true, the benevolent, the wise, is more a man, and not less, than the fool and knave. There is no tax on the good of virtue; for that is the incoming of God himself, or absolute existence, without any comparative. Material good has its tax, and if it came without desert or sweat, has no root in me, and the next wind will blow it away. But all the good of nature is the soul's, and may be had, if paid for in nature's lawful coin, that is, by labor which the heart and the head allow. I no longer wish to meet a good I do not earn, for example, to find a pot of buried gold, knowing that it brings with it new burdens. I do not wish more external goods,—neither possessions, nor honors, nor powers, nor persons. The gain is apparent; the tax is certain. But there is no tax on the knowledge that the compensation exists, and that it is not desirable to dig up treasure. Herein I rejoice with a serene eternal peace. I contract the boundaries of possible mischief. I learn the wisdom of St. Bernard,—"Nothing can work me damage except myself;

the harm that I sustain I carry about with me, and never am a real sufferer but by my own fault."

In the nature of the soul is the compensation for the inequalities of condition. The radical tragedy of nature seems to be the distinction of More and Less. How can Less not feel the pain; how not feel indignation or malevolence towards More? Look at those who have less faculty, and one feels sad, and knows not well what to make of it. He almost shuns their eye; he fears they will upbraid God. What should they do? It seems a great injustice. But see the facts nearly, and these mountainous inequalities vanish. Love reduces them, as the sun melts the iceberg in the sea. The heart and soul of all men being one, this bitterness of *His* and *Mine* ceases. His is mine. I am my brother, and my brother is me. If I feel overshadowed and outdone by great neighbors, I can yet love; I can still receive; and he that loveth maketh his own the grandeur he loves. Thereby I make the discovery that my brother is my guardian, acting for me with the friendliest designs, and the estate I so admired and envied is my own. It is the nature of the soul to appropriate all things. Jesus and Shakespeare are fragments of the soul, and by love I conquer and incorporate them in my own conscious domain. His virtue,—is not that mine? His wit,—if it cannot be made mine, it is not wit.

Such, also, is the natural history of calamity. The changes which break up at short intervals the prosperity of men are advertisements of a nature whose law is growth. Every soul is by this intrinsic necessity quitting its whole system of things, its friends, and home, and laws, and faith, as the shell-fish crawls out of its beautiful but stony case, because it no longer admits of its growth, and slowly forms a new house. In proportion to the vigor of the individual, these revolutions are frequent, until in some happier mind they are incessant, and all worldly relations hang very loosely about him, becoming, as it were, a transparent fluid membrane through which the living form is seen, and not, as in most men, an indurated heterogeneous fabric of many dates, and of no settled character in which the man is imprisoned. Then there can be enlargement, and the man of today scarcely recognizes the man of yesterday. And such should be the outward biography of man in time, a putting off of dead circumstances day by day, as he renews his raiment day by day. But to us, in our lapsed estate, resting, not advancing, resisting, not cooperating with the divine expansion, this growth comes by shocks.

We cannot part with our friends. We cannot let our angels go. We do not see that they only go out, that archangels may come in. We are idolaters of the old. We do not believe in the riches of the soul, in its proper eternity and omnipresence. We do not believe there is any force in today to rival or recreate that beautiful yesterday. We linger in the ruins of the old tent, where once we had bread and shelter and organs, nor believe that the spirit can feed, cover, and nerve us again. We cannot again find aught so dear, so sweet, so graceful. But we sit and weep in vain. The voice of the Almighty saith, 'Up and onward for evermore!' We cannot stay amid the ruins. Neither will we rely on the new; and so we walk ever with reverted eyes, like those monsters who look backwards.

And yet the compensations of calamity are made apparent to the understanding also, after long intervals of time. A fever, a mutilation, a cruel disappointment, a loss of wealth, a loss of friends, seems at the moment unpaid loss, and unpayable. But the sure years reveal the deep remedial force that underlies all facts. The death of a dear friend, wife, brother, lover, which seemed nothing but privation, somewhat later assumes the aspect of a guide or genius; for it commonly operates revolutions in our way of life, terminates an epoch of infancy or of youth which was waiting to be closed, breaks up a wonted occupation, or a household, or style of living, and allows the formation of new ones more friendly to the growth of character. It permits or constrains the formation of new acquaintances, and the reception of new influences that prove of the first importance to the next years; and the man or woman who would have remained a sunny garden-flower, with no room for its roots and too much sunshine for its head, by the falling of the walls and the neglect of the gardener, is made the banian of the forest, yielding shade and fruit to wide neighborhoods of men.

Emerson's Keys to Success

Men are wiser than they know.

For every thing you have missed, you have gained something else; and for every thing you gain, you lose something.

If you tax too high, the revenue will yield nothing.

Every act rewards itself.

A man cannot speak but he judges himself.

You cannot do wrong without suffering wrong.

In labor as in life there can be no cheating. The thief steals from himself.

Love, and you shall be loved.

Our strength grows out of our weakness.

The soul refuses limits, and always affirms an Optimism, never a Pessimism.

"Nothing can work me damage except myself; the harm that I sustain I carry about with me, and never am a real sufferer but by my own fault."

WWW.SUCCESSBOOKS.NET
Visit us online for free books and more!

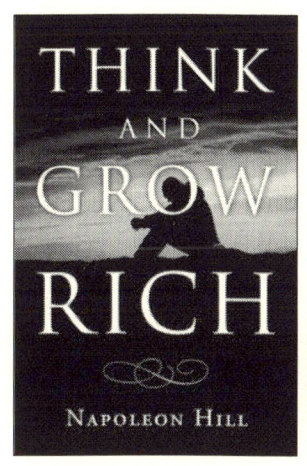

Think and Grow Rich
by Napoleon Hill

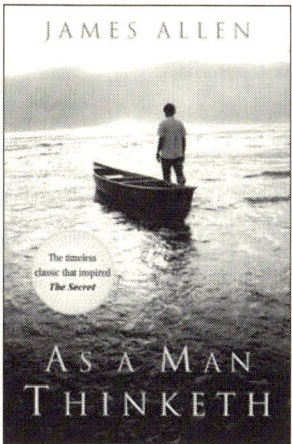

As a Man Thinketh
by James Allen

The Science of Getting Rich
by Wallace D. Wattles

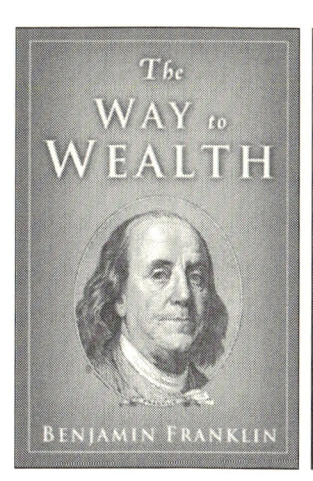

The Way to Wealth
by Benjamin Franklin

A Message to Garcia
by Elbert Hubbard

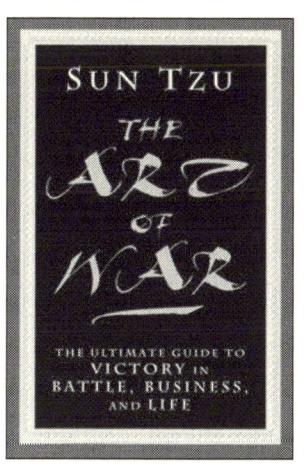

The Art of War
by Sun Tzu

Printed in Great Britain
by Amazon.co.uk, Ltd.,
Marston Gate.